WITH COURAGE AND COMPASSION

WITH COURAGE AND COMPASSION

WOMEN AND THE ECUMENICAL MOVEMENT

Aruna Gnanadason

FORTRESS PRESS

MINNEAPOLIS

WITH COURAGE AND COMPASSION:
WOMEN AND THE ECUMENICAL MOVEMENT

Paperback ISBN: 978-1-5064-3024-9

eBook ISBN: 978-1-5064-3025-6

Cover image: iStock © 2019; Rain Man Stock Illustration by DenKuvaiev

Cover design: Alisha Lofgren

Dedicated with love to
Jonathan Nallaram
Karthik Dayalan
and
Raphael
Gnanadason

CONTENTS

PREFACE

The history of women in the World Council of Churches (WCC) is an amazing mosaic of stories of courage, commitment, patient endurance and of the restless desire for revitalization, transformation, and of hope. As we look to the next phase of this history, many challenges remain. It has been a long struggle to ensure that women are represented in decision making bodies and in the staffing of the WCC—more needs to be done. At the same time, efforts continue to ensure that women's gifts and contributions are recognized in various ministries of the churches locally and nationally. Women's access to economic, social and political power in society has been an elusive dream and this needs to be continuously pursued. It is strong networks of women and others who are often the excluded at the global, the national and the regional level that keep the ecumenical movement alive. What has to be done now is for women to harness all the energy we have to offer, with greater boldness toward exploring new ways of being a community of women; and a community of women and men in church and society.

This book is not intended to provide either a chronological or factual record of the history of women in the ecumenical movement—such records are described more completely and are available elsewhere. I refer to these sources in this book and in the bibliography. This account will give a glimpse into some of the major milestones in the work related to women of the WCC; and the leadership the WCC has offered to the member churches and the ecumenical movement in challenging the churches to stand in solidarity with women. More importantly, the book underlines how the WCC has been inspired by women, who are in most places treading boldly into thus far male preserves thus creating history; engaging in the lives of their communities, in struggles for justice and dignity and a violence free world.

As is repeated several times in these pages, the ecumenical movement and the WCC in particular, has gone ahead of the churches to recognize and create the climate for greater participation of women—ensuring the availability of human and financial resources, whenever possible. It is also true that there have been times when women have faced obstacles and difficulties on the way—this book discusses a few of those moments.

The focus is on how we as women can build among ourselves a greater community—learning how to overcome regional, racial and generational divides; but more importantly by recognizing the wealth of theological, spiritual and ecclesial gifts that are brought to the table from our diverse church traditions. By learning how to respect and understand each other and appreciate the wealth of each other's heritage, while sharing our own, we will grow in unity and truly become a community of hospitality and love.

To the ecumenical movement we express gratitude, for the many ways in which the WCC and other ecumenical bodies have created safe spaces and possibilities for women to give of their best for transformation and renewal. While this book concentrates on the history of women in the World Council of Churches; this is not the legacy of the WCC alone. Partner organizations such as the World YWCA, the World Communion of Reformed Churches and the Lutheran World Federation among others, have done exceedingly well on this agenda—collaborative work is visible throughout, with a common commitment to the search for justice; and for a compassionate church and world. To this number can be added international ecumenical organizations such as the World Day of Prayer movement and the Fellowship of the Least Coin movement as well as the women's programs of the regional ecumenical organizations, of national councils of churches and of many individual churches—they have all made important contributions to women globally. The secular women's movement in all our countries, movements of women of other faiths nationally and globally; and the community of feminist theologians continue to inspire us and walk with us in our search for a more just world.

The issues I have chosen to address in this book are not the only ones that have preoccupied the minds of women in the

WCC, nor are they intended to be the complete or final word on these concerns—I hope the discussions in the book will provoke women, even inspire those who are active in the ecumenical movement and in the churches, to consider how we can move forward in our search for justice and dignity for all women. There is much that still needs to be addressed and done. This text affirms the range of women's dreams and aspirations formed by various social locations, nourished by diverse spiritualities, with theological resources from different church traditions. The reflections and analysis are personal and autobiographical at points as I weave together voices and opinions of women from all over the world with my own. I have briefly referred to the past, but my concentration is on the last few decades leading up to the Ninth Assembly of the WCC in Porto Alegre, 2006.

I hope this book will give birth to new directions in the work the WCC does on women in the context of injustice, increasing violence and the onslaughts on the integrity of creation in our world today. The importance of a strong WCC and the continuing commitments of the ecumenical movement to women and to justice and peace cannot be stressed enough.

Aruna Gnanadason
Chennai, India

WORDS OF GRATITUDE

My heartfelt gratitude to all the women who feature in this book—to all the women named and unnamed, who are part of this shared history of women and the ecumenical movement, women who tirelessly work in their churches and communities, too often unrecognized, even ignored. A personal thanks to all the women who gave their time to either speak to me or write to me and to all those who have had an influence on me and have made the WCC's work meaningful. I have been asked who I am addressing in this book—without hesitation, I would say it is the women in the ecumenical movement, those who have gone before us; those whose memories live on through their contributions; and present and future generations of ecumenists.

My thanks to the two general secretaries of the WCC under whom I worked—Rev. Dr Konrad Raiser and Rev. Dr Sam Kobia—the conversations I had with them helped me sharpen what I should write about. They created the environment for me to concentrate on the research for this book and supported me—for all this my thanks. With them, several women in the staff leadership team past and present encouraged and walked with me—to them my gratitude. My staff colleagues in the WCC women's program and the justice, peace and creation team and their passion and commitment to keep these inter-related issues squarely on the agenda of the WCC has been inspirational.

Special thanks to the women in the governing bodies of the WCC, who have worked tirelessly, sometimes through the night to strategize, to draft statements or resolutions, to inform each other, or mentor younger women—to represent the concerns of women in decision making places to ensure that the WCC stays on track in its commitments to women. This has often been fun filled and joyous, but sometimes tough too but their patience has most often paid off.

I also say thanks to the United Church of Canada, especially to Patti Talbot, Michael Blair, Omega Bula and Heather Spares for the invitation to be the Anne Duncan Gray Scholar for the autumn term of 2014, endorsed by the Asian Women's Resource Centre. This three-month period, being immersed in the wealth of relevant books and materials in the library of the Emmanuel College in Toronto, under the care of Karen Wishart, the librarian; and having scintillating conversations with Lois Wilson, Marilyn Legge and Lynda Katsuno and a host of others who had been part of WCC's history, set the tone for me to work on this book. After several interruptions, I could come back to it in earnest only very recently. It has been an honor to work on this personal testimony of gratitude to the life and work of the WCC and to ecumenical women globally.

I thank Ranjini Rebera, Marilyn Legg, Lois Wilson, Janice Love and Margot Käßmann, my friends and long-time ecumenical partners for reading parts of the manuscript and for their valuable suggestions for improvements. To Jesudas Athyal, Acquiring Editor, South Asian Theology, Fortress Press, and the team he works with who arranged for this publication, my appreciation for creating the possibility for me to write this book. A special word of thanks to Jesudas who accompanied the process throughout, sending me gentle reminders to get the manuscript completed.

To Mallika Badrinath, my younger sister for the meaningful artwork and design for the cover of the book—she always provides the most fitting designs.

To my family—Jonathan my husband, who knew I was writing this book and gave me all the encouragement I needed but unfortunately passed away in 2013; to my sons Chittaranjan and Uday, my daughter-in-law Daphne, my sister-in-law Nalatham and her family; and to my sisters and brothers and their families— who have all embraced me with love and care all these years—thank you. Finally, a special word of thanks to my grandsons, Karthik (nine) and Raphael (five), who teach me every day the value of an enquiring mind, creativity and imagination.

CHAPTER 1

WOMEN CREATING PLACES OF HOSPITALITY FOR HUMAN FLOURISHING

We will take the risk of dreaming dreams and sharing one another's pain. We will learn how to analyze the root-causes of the many forms of oppression of women in our communities and address them in well planned actions. We will search for the wells of living water within our communities and traditions, wells that are hidden but can be rediscovered as sources of solidarity, persistency, imagination and faith.

Anna Karin Hammar[1]

It is not a surprise that when tracing a part of the history of women in the ecumenical movement and more specifically in the World Council of Churches (WCC), I begin by remembering some of the amazing women around the world who have made significant and visible contributions to the lives of their own people and to women globally. Many of the women who are named in these pages and whose stories and struggles are recorded I have personally met during my travels on behalf of the WCC or in other work related to the women's program of the WCC. The power of women in different countries, regions and denominations has without a doubt, influenced the WCC in shaping its work. The WCC, since its inception in 1948, has been committed to women and has invested resources and personnel to ensure that women can contribute their best to church and society, and that their struggles for justice and dignity find responses.

1

In fact, the WCC, as a movement, went ahead of individual churches in giving dignity and voice to women by affirming the vision of church as a just community of women and men. "Long before many member churches showed an interest in the man/woman debate, the WCC had taken it seriously. It had spent time, money, and effort in facing the difficulties and providing forums in which pioneer thinking could evolve."[2] Likewise, the critical solidarity of women with the ecumenical movement has ensured that new and difficult challenges are addressed boldly and are creatively dealt with in ecumenical debates and actions. While there are hundreds of women one can name and write about in this account, just a few are remembered in these pages to give a glimpse of how women have used their skills and the forms of resistance open to them, to affirm life. But first, let us journey around the world to meet some of the women who have crossed the path of the WCC's women's program in recent years.

IF YOU BUT DARE TOUCH MY SON!

"Stubborn, insistent, determined"—these are the words that my pastor used at the Easter morning service,[3] to describe the unshakable presence of Mary Magdalene at the empty tomb on that early Easter morning (Mark 16:1-11). Mary refused to leave the grave, even after the disciples had scattered in fear. She was not ready to accept that Jesus was no longer with them. It is this stubbornness, insistence and determination that I saw in the face of Mariam[4] in Beit Sahour, a town Southeast of Bethlehem in Palestine. Mariam lives in that home, with her husband. Her daughters live with their families in that same town. Mariam's unstinting commitment to her people and to her family, her strong eyes, her capable hands and her warm heart are etched in my memory. Mariam's story is not very different from that of the 50,000 or so Palestinian Christians who remain in the Holy Land. Every day is a struggle. Every time she tries to travel to Jerusalem from Beit Sahour, she is not sure how she will be treated by the young Israeli soldiers who manage one of the 6000 checkpoints that control the movement of her people. Mariam shared with us the story of her obstinate resilience, against all odds, to get her sons out of the country so that they could continue their studies abroad in peace, rather than living in constant fear. For her, this meant dodging through checkpoints, begging Israeli soldiers for permission to pass through and even keeping silent when one of the officers misread the passport and the visa and assumed that her sons were already students in a foreign country. "I told myself that I will not allow them to do anything to my sons. I was ready to even bite the soldier if he dared to touch my son," she told us when we met her in March 2009.[5]

It is no wonder then that Teresa, her daughter is equally gutsy! Teresa's life too is riddled with the daily struggles under Occupation. She is a senior theatre nurse in the neonatal intensive care unit of the Bethlehem Hospital. It was at the time of the siege of Bethlehem, in 2002, that Teresa was to deliver her own twin babies. Getting to the hospital was a horrendous experience in itself—fortunately a brief lifting of the curfew helped. Being a neonatal nurse and knowing that the siege had ensured that a necessary lifesaving drug was not immediately available kept her extremely worried, despite the doctors' assurances that they will do all they can to get the drug to her if needed. Her mother, who had to dodge the curfew to reach her in hospital, was another cause for anxiety for Teresa. It was therefore a great relief that all went well and the twins—a girl and a boy—were safely born.

Teresa shared with us another encounter she had with the authorities. She was trying to travel to East Jerusalem as she had promised to get to the church to help with setting it up for a celebration. She had the necessary permit to pass through the checkpoint—but this time it was not possible, because the checkpoints were closed due to the Jewish festival of Purim.[6] As she had committed herself to help in the church, she opted to make a huge detour to reach another checkpoint that is often less used, hoping that it will not be guarded. It all looked well, and she thought she had made it through, only to be stopped by a soldier who was standing behind a building. She appealed to him, literally begged him to let her through explaining the reason for her need to get to the other side. He took her travel authorization permit from her, and she stood expectantly thinking she had made an impact on him. He came back, returned her document and repeated that the checkpoint was closed, and she could not get through. A dejected Teresa returned home disappointed.

3

Teresa's story did not end on a note of resignation. A few months later, she went to renew her permit to enter Jerusalem and was refused. She asked why and was told that there was a mark against her name in official records, indicating that she was a terrorist—this is what the soldier had done on the earlier date, when he had taken her document from her. She ran from pillar to post trying to undo the damage—she needed to have the permit, not least because of her desire to worship in Jerusalem. One day, after yet another refusal, at one of the army offices, she sat dejected on a bench outside, wondering what she could do. Suddenly a young man wearing a distinctive vest came up to her and asked her if he could help. She shared with him her story. He asked her to wait for a moment—he called the offices of Rabbis for Human Rights (an Israeli solidarity group). The person on the other end of the line advised her of the steps she should take, to renew her permit.

When Teresa had completed her story, I asked her who the man was who had so helpfully come to her rescue. It turned out to be an Ecumenical Accompanier from the Ecumenical Accompaniment Program in Palestine and Israel (EAPPI). It warmed my heart to hear that a project of the churches in Jerusalem, in which the WCC is a partner and was involved and instrumental in setting up, had been the angel of mercy. Of course, there are many, many more Palestinians who need such support and accompaniment, in a context of the daily struggle to just live, move, work, and worship in freedom. Will peace and justice ever come to this land torn apart for over sixty years? This story of the courage of women struggling and surviving in the Occupied Territories is one story of women from around the world who with resilience and acts of subversive resistance, work for transformation.

We refuse to be enemies

Many Palestinian groups are peacefully resisting the Occupation. Among them is the Nassar family of Palestinian Christians, who have owned forty two hectares of land south-west of Bethlehem since 1924. In 1991, they learned that the Israeli government was planning to confiscate the land. Since then, the Nassar family has been locked in a costly legal battle with the Israeli government, despite them having in their possession all the land registration documents and other paperwork necessary to prove their legal ownership of the land. So far, the family has spent some $140,000 in legal fees trying to protect the land from confiscation. One of the sons explains to us that along with the huge financial cost to his family over the past eighteen years, they have endured attacks from nearby Israeli settlers, who uprooted 250 olive trees from their land, and had threatened his mother with a gun. Despite this, the family made an important decision—that rather than respond violently, or pack up and leave, they would *refuse to be enemies*. This slogan is proudly proclaimed at the entrance to the farm and has formed the basis of the *Tent of Nations* project that they have started on their land. This peace-building project invites young people from all over the world to visit the Nassar family's land, to keep the land alive and help them to protect it from confiscation. Visitors get involved in tree-planting, olive picking, art projects, and other activities. Summer camps for children from Bethlehem are designed to re-connect children with the land.

Israeli solidarity groups

Rabbis for Human Rights, referred to earlier, is one among the small but strong initiatives of Jews in Israel, and in other parts of the world, who oppose the policies of the Israeli government and support Palestinians—at great personal cost. There are many Jewish groups, working for justice and peace (some within the frame of Zionism) but all demanding that the human and other rights of Palestinians be respected and honored. Among the groups we heard about were: Peace Now, Bat Shalom, Women in Black, "Civil"ization, Women for Peace, among others. We met with representatives of the Israeli Committee against House Demolitions and visited Silwan, one of the places where the Committee was joining hands with Palestinian groups to oppose the demolition of houses by Israeli forces to forcibly take over the land—the houses were being demolished to extend a park around the City of David. The founder of the organization against demolitions, Jeff Halper, has written a powerful book titled, *An Israeli in Palestine: Resisting Dispossession, Redeeming Israel*. We also met and had conversations with Rabbi Daniel Rossing (from the Jerusalem Centre for Jewish Christian Relations) and Rabbi Arik Ashcherman (from Rabbis for Human Rights). Their commitment to justice and peace for the Palestinians was inspiring. But, as they themselves regretfully acknowledged, they are too few to make a strong enough impact on Jewish society.

The situation that faces many Palestinians we met has several layers of complexity. Israel has enacted an ever-tightening hold on both the land and the people within Palestine. Palestinian land has shrunk in the West Bank and Gaza now making up less than 22 percent of historic Palestine. To "protect" themselves against supposed Palestinian attacks, Israel started building a "separation barrier" in 2002, and today more than 50 percent of the wall has been constructed. It is predicted that when completed, only 13 percent of the wall will be along the Green Line,[7] and the remaining 87 percent will be inside the West Bank, violating international law and creating a situation where Israel is able to wrest more of, and the best, land and natural resources from Palestine. At the time of writing, there were 129 Israeli settlements and 438,088 Israeli settlers in the Palestinian Territories, the wall had been built to encapsulate the illegal settlements into Israel. There are currently 592 Israeli road blocks in the West Bank which cause extensive economic, medical and psychological repercussions on the Palestinian population, demonstrated by the fact that 64 percent of Palestinians live below the poverty line.

From Palestine, we travel to South Africa where we meet the next story of courageous resistance by women.

REMEMBER, YOU ARE BUT A BROKEN PIECE OF A FRAGMENTED CHURCH!

The year was 1990—it is a momentous time for South Africa. Political change was finally coming—Nelson Mandela was released in February of that year, after spending twenty-seven years in the infamous Robben Island prison. The South Africa Council of Churches (SACC) had been under constant attack and threat over the apartheid years, for the clear stand it took against apartheid and all the violence and repression that went with it. The WCC was not allowed, as an organization, to enter the country because of its strong condemnation of the system of apartheid and its support of the then African National Congress (ANC).

In that moment of political change, a wide spectrum of churches representing the SACC along with charismatic, Pentecostal, evangelical, African Independent and the Roman Catholic Church came together at a historic conference in the town of Rustenberg, some eighty kilometers outside Johannesburg. Of the 300 participants, very few were women and most of them were staff, "oiling the wheels of the conference and serving the men."[8]

I had the honor of representing the WCC at this historic event along with Pauline Webb,[9] Archbishop Kirill (now His Holiness Patriarch Kirill, the Patriarch of Moscow and all of Russia), Rev. Oscar McCloud, African-American pastor from the Presbyterian Church, USA, and Mr. James Mutambwira from Zimbabwe, then staff person in the Program to Combat Racism at the World Council of Churches. Travelling to South Africa at that time was a challenge for me, because the Indian passport clearly indicated then, that it was not valid for travel in South Africa and Israel. India was one of the first countries to officially recognize the African National Congress (ANC) and the Palestinian Liberation Organization (PLO) as legitimate political leaders of the two countries. Fortunately, this was the new South Africa, and though my passport could not have the visa stamped into it, the WCC through the South Africa Conference of Churches had organized for the visa to be issued on a separate sheet of paper on arrival, and this gave me safe passage into the country.

No doubt the conference was being organized in difficult times and attempting to bring the churches together across racial and theological divides was no mean task. However, this can be no excuse for what happened to women at that conference—it is symptomatic of what happens once too often in the church and the ecumenical movement. After intense lobbying by women and youth, it had been agreed that there would be one hour set aside on the final evening of the conference for the women to voice their concerns.

Two women were brought in from Johannesburg to address the conference. Sheena Duncan, one of the speakers, recollects:

> When we took our places on the platform at the appointed time, a delegate took up the floor microphone and addressed the assembling crowd to the effect that this session was a waste of the time of the conference and not a priority at a gathering such as this one. It was apparent that most of the representatives agreed with him, so we walked out accompanied by most of the women present in the hall.[10]

As a privileged visitor to that conference, this event will stay in my memory forever. The speaker from the floor, who in fact did not even wait for the official opening of the session nor sought the moderator's permission to take the floor, considered that the final communiqué of the conference which had been distributed that evening was more important than the "women's session." He asked that the time be taken instead to discuss the document. On hearing this, after a moment of consultation, the three women on the dais—the Moderator of the session, Virginia Gcabashe, and the two speakers, Deborah Maboletse and Sheena Duncan—walked off the stage and out of the hall, in protest. And, with clockwork precision, almost every other woman in the hall joined the women outside to show our distress at what had happened at the gathered assembly. The soon to be declared Nobel Laureate, Archbishop Desmond Tutu then the Archbishop of Johannesburg, followed the women out and begged us to not go away without addressing the audience. Dr. Frank Chikane, the then General Secretary of the SACC, in the meantime got up to appeal to the largely male audience left there to consider the events that had occurred in that hall and to give the stage to the women. The women finally agreed to return.

Sheena Duncan, who was first called on to speak, decided to cut out most of her prepared speech, as women did not want to take up more than the allotted time, she told the audience. She said that she had intended to speak of "male control of the church over its material resources and decision making bodies," but after saying the following powerful and brief words, she sat down.

> Far, far worse than male domination of decision making and financial control, is the matter of justice; it is a fact that we as women are often made to feel that the spiritual resources of the church and the capability of theological reflection is also

an exclusive male preserve.... God is the Word. God made us in the "own image" of the Word. God made us male and female. To deny this is to deny the wholeness of God's creation. This conference is incomplete—it is a broken piece of God's Church.[11]

Deborah Maboletse, the other speaker, spoke similarly and as briefly.

Like Sheena, I don't think that perhaps after what has gone on, I should go on with some of the issues that I wanted to raise. . . .I'll ask you to forgive me. I feel emotional. But this is what I want to emphasize. I believe that with competent skills, that you folks, you Christian males have, you have a chance of contributing to this united witness for the church. But similarly, I want to warn you that the witness is not complete without the participation of women of the church. It will succeed when women are also handling authority issues, even in a conference like this one.[12]

And the question remains—did the struggle to overcome apartheid have an impact on all power relations in South Africa? As an online article on Women's Net, posted early in 2010, describes it:

In practical terms, the dominant anti-apartheid nature of those struggles ensured that the economic and socio-cultural "sides" of the gendered oppression equation were effectively sidelined. When the apartheid state was "captured," the inherited relations of power, production and distribution were not, outside of a subsequent elite-led de-racialization, altered in any significant way—thus transferring the core character of an apartheid patriarchal capitalism into a new post-apartheid patriarchal capitalism. Despite all the good intentions, fine rhetoric, myriad events and work done, the intervening decade has seen a precipitous rise in the overall levels of violence against women. The often cyclical and self-serving debates around rape statistics aside, the fact of the matter is that South Africa has an epidemic of violence against women. Even if many people in our country are probably "aware" that this is the case, such awareness remains stillborn as long as there is no foundational analysis and explanation of the epidemic upon which it can be tackled and fought.[13]

The phenomenal power of women can still be seen in South Africa as they take the lead in challenging patriarchal institutions, including the church.

INCREDIBLE COURAGE AND FAITH

We go to another part of the African continent and to the power of a woman of great courage and perseverance who will not be silenced. Nothing can stop the feisty Micheline Kamba Kasongo from the Democratic Republic of Congo (DRC). She does not hesitate to speak out with passion and commitment for justice. An attack of polio, as a child, had only propelled Micheline forward to take control of her life. As an ordained woman of the Church of Christ in Congo-Presbyterian Community of Kinshasa, DRC, Micheline has had her share of difficulties in a church which has struggled to survive in a war-torn country. She poignantly describes what it has meant to her and her ministry to be disabled.

> My experience as a young woman with disability influenced the most my spiritual life and my calling into the ministry. It was so difficult to be accepted as God's creation. At a teenager, I was wondering about my physical state. I attempted many times to commit suicide, but I had not succeeded. One day, my sister knew that I was planning to kill myself and she came to me and said, "My dear sister, what you want to do is not a solution of your problems. Pray and ask God what life means to you as a young lady with disability, and why God likes you to remain like this." These words from my sister were very powerful and I became conscious of my situation. I prayed, cried and implored God to teach me what the sense of my life is. That time was a healing time for me. Since that time, I have never prayed to God to heal me physically. I accepted my condition as a woman with disability and knew that God had a good plan for me. The experience of self-awareness of my physical situation as I mentioned above influenced not only my spiritual life, but also my calling into ministry. I understood my vocation to minister to people with disabilities, to encourage them to "rise up and walk" so that they can be independent and full of life to transform their situation both in Church and society.[14]

When there was hesitance from the WCC to respond to the complex political, economic and cultural realities of the DRC and of the churches there, it was Micheline's persistence that her country not be forgotten, during debates at several meetings of the WCC's Central Committee that finally triggered a much needed, major ecumenical team visit to the DRC. As she said in a presentation at the Central Committee, 2009 in Geneva, "I have realized that by sharing our sufferings, our oppressions, and our resistance to exploitation—we can also show our faith and hope in God that one day peace and justice will reign in the DRC."[15]

The WCC was compelled to make a powerful official statement about increasing sexual violence against women in the DRC. I discuss more of this later in the book, but include here a section of the Central Committee statement which recognizes that

> all protective mechanisms have failed to combat the increasing sexual violence against women in the DRC, urgent measures have to be taken by various actors to prevent this dehumanization in that country. The survivors of sexual violence in the DRC need moral support to heal their wounds, to overcome gender-based discrimination and the continuous threat to their life and security. WCC member churches, civil society organizations, the Congolese government and the international community have responsibilities to address this concern.[16]

Therefore, member churches were urged to continue to offer solidarity to the women of the DRC, through specifically the women's department of Micheline's church, the Eglise du Christ au Congo (ECC), to develop vocational training for victims so that they can sustain themselves. It appealed to the government of the DRC to guarantee the security of all the citizens of the country and particularly to protect women and girls from all forms of sexual violence. It also called on all parties to the armed conflict to immediately commit to putting an end to all acts of sexual violence against women and girls in the DRC, and to end the ongoing war.

There is hope! Amidst all the violence in the DRC, we see once again the unstinting power of women. Women of the DRC came together, again, to say "enough is enough!" The Congolese Women's Campaign against Sexual Violence in the DRC was an initiative launched by women's associations in the eastern part of the DRC to bolster the fight against sexual violence. As the petition launched by this campaign described it, "Massive displacements, arbitrary assassinations, pillage, torture, kidnapping and a still undetermined number of rapes, but a certainty that war, once again, is being waged on the bodies of women and girls." This campaign is supported by over fifty women's organizations in North and South Kivu, eastern DRC, Province Orientale, and Maniema in the Democratic Republic of the Congo—women from the churches are part of this effort. The number of organizations that have been set up in different parts of the country is indicative of the determination of women to continue to struggle.

From Africa we move to Asia and India, where 84.3 million indigenous peoples live. We meet Narango in Koraput, a small town nestled in the Eastern Ghats in India (the mountain range on the eastern part of the country.)

Determination to Protect the Earth, Our Mother

Narango Pujari is a Kond, which is an indigenous tribe in Orissa, in Central India. During my visit there, she said to me, "We may die, we may face death, but we will not leave the land—we will not be separated from our mother." Narango is a woman leader of the Deomali Adivasi Mahila Sangh, in Koraput, Orissa.[17] Deomali is a mountain on the Eastern Ghats of India, in Orissa. It is covered by lush green forests and shrubbery. Many medicinal plants grow there. It is considered sacred by the indigenous peoples who live there. It is constantly under threat of being "developed" into a tourist resort by the government. The organization of indigenous women took their sacred mountain's name in their title as they join hands with the indigenous men to stop the destruction of their ancestral lands in the name of development.

Narango speaks powerfully of humanity's connection to the earth. She said, "Life starts on the land for the woman, from the moment she is born. She wakes up each day on the land and the rivers, trees, birds are also living on the land—they are all our relatives." She continued, "There is a relationship between the woman and the land—that is why we begin cultivating the land only after we worship the mother, i.e. the earth."[18]

She, as an indigenous woman, spoke of the earth as mother, in a relational sense, but, there is no space for romanticism here. Indigenous women too face violence in the domestic sphere, as mothers and as women. In my dialogue with Narango, her reference to the selfless love that the earth as mother has for all her children did not have patriarchal overtones. Narango said, in a very matter-of-fact way, that the

> earth is like our mother, like a mother who cares for her children selflessly. The earth cares for our needs selflessly. As humans we go through the life cycle—we give birth, we nurture our young ones at the breast, we grow up and we die. The earth will never die, but this requires that we as women who go through the same processes of birthing and caring for our children need to also nurture the earth.[19]

She was also pragmatic in her explanation as to why they consider some groves and mountains to be sacred. "The sacred groves are seed banks—and have a diversity of plants. Therefore, we worship them. We never touch this life source, and allow regeneration there. In this way the sustainability of the earth is protected."[20] The setting aside of some spaces as sacred has ensured the long-term sustainability of resources and has religious and customary practices associated with it. Narango ended by saying, "We may die, we may face death, but we will not leave the land—we will not be separated from our mother."[21]

To Narango, there is power in the relational and "sacrificial" value of motherhood, debunking it of the expectations patriarchy has imposed on it. The social scientists and activists, Maria Mies and Vandana Shiva agree that,

> for Third World women who fight for the conservation of their survival base this spiritual icing-on-the-cake, the divorce of the spiritual from the material is incomprehensible for them. The term Mother Earth does not need to be qualified by inverted commas, because they regard the earth as a living being, which guarantees their own and all their fellow creatures' survival. They respect and celebrate earth's sacredness and resist its transformation into dead, raw material for industrialism and commodity production. It follows, therefore, that they also respect both the diversity and the limits of nature which cannot be violated if they want to survive.[22]

Despite all their determination and struggles, indigenous peoples in India (who refer to themselves as Adivasis or Tribals) are slowly losing control over their lands which they had cared for and lived on for centuries. They constitute 8 percent of India's population and yet form a major large section of all displaced people due to "development" projects.[23] Orissa, a central Indian state, where deforestation, mining and industrialization are putting the lives of the indigenous people at risk, has also gone through serious natural disasters in recent years—in 1999, Orissa experienced one of the world's most devastating killer cyclones. In 2001, it was struck by one of the worst droughts in history and later that year, during the monsoon season, it experienced another destructive flood. Floods, droughts and dramatic climatic changes and the threats to the lives of the peoples who live on the land, are linked to the imprudent use of the resources of the earth. Women like Narango are determined to keep up the resistance. The treatment meted out to indigenous peoples in India as elsewhere in the world is a form of racism—they have been denied their right to survive by interference in their way of life and livelihood. The WCC partners with indigenous peoples through a program dedicated to them. This has been done in conjunction with the work on overcoming racism. In this, Marilia Alves Schuller, an Afro-Brazilian woman, has played a pivotal role.

PASSIONATE AND COMPASSIONATE IN RESISTING RACISM AND CASTEISM

The passion and compassion with which Marilia Alves Schuller continues to participate in the life of the ecumenical movement and in the struggles of indigenous women, women of African descent, Dalit women and women from ethnic minority groups, makes her a precious gift to the world. She embodies in her life choices, and in her relationships with all she encounters, the power of the women's movement in church and society and the power of her own faith. In her work as a woman of African descent, she demonstrates that women living under racism and casteism have a transforming world view to offer. Marilia's own feminist consciousness is positioned at the intersection of racism and women's struggles for justice and dignity.

In Brazil, women of African descent such as Marilia, place the roots of their movement in the post-slavery era when former slaves started to organize themselves. The early twentieth century witnessed important achievements in this regard, including the formation of the first association of Brazilian female domestic workers in 1936 in Santos, São Paulo, and the 1950 inaugural convention of the National Council of Black Women in São Paulo. The 1970s represented a moment of considerable expansion—the establishment of links with international feminism had a great impact on women in Brazil. At the 1975 Brazilian Women's Congress held in Rio de Janeiro, delegations of Afro-Brazilian women denounced racial and sexual discrimination. By the early twenty-first century, there were many nongovernmental Afro-Brazilian women's organizations, with the important ones located in the cities of São Paulo, Rio de Janeiro, and Bahia. Increasingly autonomous women's groups came into existence among black women because the predominantly white mainline feminist movement or the black people's movements too did not pay sufficient attention to the race, gender, and class specificities of black women.[24]

Marilia writes that it was participation in the ecumenical movement that made her aware of her own identity and she acquired the necessary elements to analyze the situation of her own people in Brazil.

> I started to understand my story as a black woman in a collective sense. The stories of other black women and men in other parts of the world were interconnected with mine. We had a common history, that of colonialism, slavery, slave trade, abolition of slavery and the lack of real conditions for assimilation into society. The present situation of the Black People in Brazil remains inextricably related to that history. It is a history of racism and inequalities, of which we are survivors. New developments—like recognition of ancestral Black communities' territories and affirmative action policies—now in existence for a few decades are slowly improving the life conditions of Black People.[25]

Speaking about racism and casteism has never been easy—the churches hesitate to recognize these as sins that scar the life of the churches and nations. There was enthusiasm when the struggle was against apartheid in South Africa—this felt like it was someone else's problem for which solidarity was sought. The member churches of the WCC contributed generously to overcome apartheid—but then when new forms of racism, or the ongoing struggles of people of African descent or of Dalits was discussed, it was not so easy—perhaps because it challenges us to acknowledge the racism and casteism in our own context and in our own churches. And yet, the work on overcoming racism and casteism and in accompanying indigenous peoples in their struggles for their ways of life, their languages, and most of all for their lands and their sovereignty continued at the global level—both at the level of the United Nations and at the WCC. More importantly, it grew at local levels in each place where racism/casteism had splintered people and has endowed some with privilege. Through a program entitled Just and Inclusive Communities, the WCC continued to mobilize the churches to work with vigor on exposing the continuing racism against peoples of African descent. Movements of those affected have become strong and the people define the needs and strategies for their struggles to make the churches take on their responsibility to overcome racism and casteism. It is therefore appropriate to next meet Annathaie Abhayasekara in Sri Lanka—a woman of daunting courage who continued to do her work even as a civil war was raging around her in her small island nation.

Unrelenting Energy and Commitment

She now uses a walking stick and is on regular insulin injections, but Annathaie Abhayasekara[26] cannot be stopped. She asks me to meet her in the picturesque little town of Hatton nestled among verdant tea plantations along undulating hills in what is called the "Up Country" in Sri Lanka. From Hatton we drive along a road leading toward Sri Pada, or Adam's Peak (which is the English name for one of the tallest mountains in Sri Lanka). Sri Pada or in Sinhala, "God's feet," is so called because Christians believe it has the imprint of Adam's foot on it. The Buddhists also revere this mountain as they believe it is the Buddha's footprint while the Hindus believe it is the footprint of the Lord Shiva. The beauty and grandeur of the mountains make them truly an abode of the gods. It is near this sacred mountain that Annathaie's work with plantation women workers has been going on for the past thirty-four years. She is "retiring" from this work, she tells me, as she is proudly handing it over to a bright young group of women.

As we walk through the beautiful tea plantations in Hatton, Sri Lanka, in 2010, she tells me the story of the plantation women workers as an illustration of the triple oppression of a group of women based on race, class and gender anchored in a patriarchal society. The tea industry is now firmly in the grip of owners of the plantations, as part of Lanka's colonial legacy. Annathaie began her work with the plantation women in a modest way to raise the awareness of the women to their triple oppression and to provide them a space to organize themselves and train themselves to contribute to their own welfare. Under the title *Penn Wimochana Gnanodayam* (PWG) (which, roughly translated from the original Tamil, is "liberation of women is possible with the dawn of wisdom"), this movement has, over the years, created a leadership of tea pickers, knowledgeable about their rights as workers and as women.

The women gather together regularly to talk of issues such as domestic violence, incest, rape, sexual harassment and alcoholism and plan strategies to deal with them. Women's health issues, including awareness about the dangers of HIV and AIDS, are also discussed. PWG has set up several pre-nursery schools for plantation children with a view to prepare them for the education system and to inculcate in them the values of their own culture. In 1985, the Hill Country Educational Foundation was established and provides scholarships to deserving girls and boys, both Tamil and Sinhala to enable them to continue their education. Along with other NGOs and church related groups, PWG contributes to discussions and joint actions on behalf of the plantation workers—in their struggles for justice and access to their rights.

The history of the *Malayaga Makkal* (Hill/Up Country Tamils) dates to these times. In the wake of a famine in India when many of the ancestors of the present generation of *Malayaga Makkal* hailing from lower caste groups faced starvation and death in South India, recruiters promised them green pastures and employment in Sri Lanka. Recruitment based on caste ensured the perpetuation of this form of social differentiation which is observed till today. The planters actively encouraged this form of traditional separation among the workers to meet the economic needs of the plantation production system. Evidence of this is seen in the demarcation of living quarters among workers along caste lines.

The Kandyan peasantry who lost their lands was hostile to the British and the workers from South India. As coffee failed and tea was introduced, the industry became labor intensive—the British opened tea plantations in the 1860s. Between 1839–1842, women comprised of only 7.55 percent of total labor migration into Sri Lanka, by 1860 they made up 33 percent of the workforce, and today this is 52 percent, with women doing the most back breaking part of the work—the picking of the leaves. These workers till today are viewed as an "immigrant group" with no claim to legitimacy, permanency or indigenousness that the other ethnic groups have claimed, leading to economic deprivation, exploitation and political marginalization. An Indian flag flutters in the wind in the Tamil settlement!

The myth of "nimble" fingers that women are supposed to possess is suitable for tasks that are intensive and repetitive—women's patience and dexterity, Annathaie tells me, is said to be the reason for this. Men are employed in the more physically demanding tasks of weeding, applying fertilizers, pruning trees etc., thus perpetuating the sexual division of labor. The patriarchal society existent in India in the 1880s was brought to Sri Lanka and is prevalent even today, nearly over one and a half centuries later! The enclave nature of the plantation set up (the workers live in barracks) did not permit socialization outside the estate. In the bygone era they had to carry a "*thundu*" (an official document) and later a ration card as an identity marker, not unlike the passes that the blacks in South Africa had to carry when they travelled from place to place. The plantation women are socialized to obey, serve and to be the property of the male members of their families. For the plantation owners of this labor-intensive industry, it made more economic sense to employ women workers, as higher profits could be extracted by paying lower wages to them. It is these experiences of working with the women in the plantations of Sri Lanka that Annathaie brought to the WCC's work on combatting racism.

We have Learned How to Use Our Power, How to Create Places of Hospitality for Human Flourishing

All the women spoken of in the above section live with courage and resistance to injustice and violence. They cannot be silenced, because backing them up are thousands of women who survive and flourish because of their solidarity with each other, across many humanly constructed divides. In the coming chapters of this book, there is information about the "women to women solidarity visits" which was a program that focused on women in countries in conflict, the Living Letters pastoral visits, and other visits that the WCC has organized over the past decades that reach out to women in all parts of the world—Sierra Leone, Liberia, the Sudan, Kenya, Indonesia, Sri Lanka, Pakistan, Croatia, Serbia, Romania, Nicaragua, Panama, Rwanda, Burundi, Colombia, Haiti, Bolivia, Palestine, Rwanda, to name just a very few. In all these places it is women who make the difference. It is their courage, their commitment to peace with justice that has changed the course of the histories of their nations—even if they so often go unrecognized and even ignored. Often male colleagues of the WCC who visit these countries would comment on the significant role women are playing, as the backbone of their families, of society and of the churches; but then by and large this stays as lip service, and apart from significant exceptions, little effort was made to ensure that women are drawn into the leadership of the churches or included in ecumenical delegations of the WCC or its programs.

Women Reshaping the Structures

And yet, it is women such as these who have inspired the work of the WCC in its programmatic responses to women. It is women such as these who have motivated the women who have served the WCC in several capacities—either in its decision making structures or as executives in the headquarters in Geneva. Women's faithfulness to the ecumenical vision is impeccable as they turn with hope to the WCC and the role it can play; and as they testify to the unique and important place of the WCC in the world today. I asked a select number of women to tell me how the WCC has impacted their lives and here are some of their responses in personal correspondence.[27]

Bärbel Wartenberg-Potter[28] is a Lutheran theologian from Germany, who retired as the Bishop of the region of Holstein Lübeck (2001-2008). She was Director of the Sub-Unit on Women in Church and Society of the WCC from 1980 to 1985. Under her care, the visibility of women was enhanced in WCC programs and governing bodies—for example in the leadership at the Sixth Assembly of the WCC in Vancouver, Canada, 1983, where women were visible, and made strong theological and other content contributions to the theme, as well as in leadership roles in every aspect of the Assembly. She also ensured that all program units of the WCC initiated activities that would high-light the impact of their work on the lives of women and would include women in all activities—an effort that continues to be sustained to a certain extent. Barbel writes,

> The WCC is indispensable to promote the vision of a world-wide church in which the gifts of all its members are used to up-build the body of Christ. The WCC makes visible, that no one church is complete or is a lone bearer of the full witness. Ecumenicity—the fact that we need each other and do not claim to have the truth alone was and is a guiding principle of my own ecclesiological conviction. The WCC must car-ry the core convictions of Galatians 3:28 forward. I do think the member churches have been acting shortsightedly in these times of economic globalization, to cut their own global mul-tilateral structures to such a small size. This is a major mistake in church history. The WCC has had to cope with its survival because of ever narrowing support, instead of bringing before the churches the burning issues of the times.[29]

Mercy Amba Oduyoye,[30] ended her long career in the ecu-menical movement and concluded at the WCC as its Deputy General Secretary, from 1987 to 1994. In 1989, she founded the Circle of Concerned African Women Theologians, a network which spans all of Africa; and the Institute of African Women in Religion and Culture at Trinity Theological Seminary in Ghana, of which she was Director. Mercy's role in the WCC was of great importance because she encouraged many of us women who were on the staff; helped us give direction to the work and spoke out boldly and strongly in support of the work with women. She was actively engaged in developing the agen-da of the Ecumenical Decade of the Churches in Solidarity with Women and continued to contribute her theological gifts to the

Women's program even after her return to Ghana. She is a prolific writer and out of all her writings, what is of importance in this context is the RISK book, *Who Will Roll the Stone Away?* (WCC:1990) which records events around the launch of the Ecumenical Decade of the Churches in Solidarity with Women (more on this later). In response to my question to her as to how the WCC had impacted her work and life, she wrote,

> I have spent a good part of my creative years, 1966-94 and after, nourished by the vision of the visible unity of the church and of Christians, with the WCC as catalyst. I have lived to see the churches abandoning the vision and going back into their denominations. What I see is lip service to the vision and that makes me sad indeed. What future do I see? I must get myself into a more positive mood to answer this. I need to pray about this as the future is in God's hands. As I see it, some of it will depend on discerning where the churches need a catalyst to make them function as the body of Christ and to provide the needed stimulus.[31]

Agnes Aboum[32] became Moderator of the WCC at the Tenth Assembly of the WCC, 2013, in Busan—the first woman and first African to be elected to this position. As we reflect on the history of women in the ecumenical movement, it will be clear that this is no mean victory for us as women, as we have failed previously when we lobbied hard to get a woman into this position. Agnes began her journey with the ecumenical movement as a young woman in 1975 at the Fifth General Assembly in Nairobi in the communications office as a co-opted staff. She was on the staff of the WCC as Associate Youth Coordinator for two years. From 1987-1998, she was advisor to the Commission on the Churches' Participation in Development, (CCPD). In 1998-2006, she was elected and served as the Africa President of the WCC. From then, she has been a member of the WCC Central Committee and Executive Committee. She played an important role in the WCC, having served on the search committee for two General Secretaries. She has been supportive of the work of the WCC on Women and Economic Justice and in all the work on Justice, Peace and the Integrity of Creation, a Commission she served on. I quote Agnes Aboum extensively, as she raises important challenges:

21

In recent times we argued over the issue of gender based and sexual violence and the role of the church as an accomplice. This is a difficult topic for some male church leaders but a bitter pill that must be swallowed if healing, reconciliation and culture of impunity and silence must be stopped within church circles. On issues of economic justice—the AGAPE[33] experience remains a thorn in the flesh because whilst South and North churches agree on causes of poverty, we are far from each other when it comes to strategies and solutions. This is perhaps an area that continues to define our North–South solidarity or lack of it. . . . In discussions on economic justice, gender was central as poverty bears the face of a woman, hence we speak of the feminization of poverty.

The most frustrating moment was in Canberra where a rape took place and instead of thinking of and empathizing with the young woman, some church leaders accused the woman of destroying the career of the man who raped her. Once again it was the victim being victimized. It was the woman who was to blame, and the poor man was innocent. Of course, he was sent home, but the damage was done, and the discussions remained within the women's caucus. It was a confirmation of the gender violence in the church that is constantly denied. Another experience was the way in which a renowned female ecumenist was unjustly treated at the Harare Assembly. Male leadership colluded to block her candidature as Moderator. This event saw two women eventually leave the WCC thereby weakening the movement and the women's voice. This remains a regrettable happening, in my view.

It is essential to note that WCC structures and work culture are outdated and cannot deliver. Structures cannot just be polished, they need an overhaul. Governance requires functioning in an accountable and transparent way. Within these structures, it is important to say that Women's Work and staff kept women alive from confusion through meetings and briefings. However, in struggles there is something called critical majority without which your impact is limited. That is what has hampered women in the WCC. We have made strides, but we are not a critical majority in numbers and reflection/action. I believe the WCC has never been as weak as now in terms of gender equity and issues.

There is a future for the WCC because it exists to respond to the call and prayer of our Lord Jesus that they may all be one. However, if the structures, work culture and gender equity remain in the state it is, then it will continue to diminish as the Vatican and the Evangelical movement gain momentum. What is our flagship for the twenty-first century? Who is the WCC in the changed global arena? What type of leadership do we require? These are questions that require objective discussions. Let us have a woman General Secretary and test the waters.[34]

Margot Käßmann[35] is another important voice for women in the WCC. She is a Lutheran theologian from Germany and was Landesbischöfin of the Evangelical-Lutheran Church of Hanover in Germany and still serves as a pastor of the church. As a member of the WCC's Central Committee and Executive Committee, she had been pivotal in ensuring that many creative programs were approved and initiated. She was nominated to serve on the Central Committee from the floor at the Sixth Assembly of the WCC in Vancouver in 1983 by youth delegates and this marked a new consciousness among youth that they had leadership gifts to offer to the ecumenical movement. Her church was not willing to give up one of the six seats they were entitled to, for a youth. To her, one of the most important WCC processes she was involved in programmatically was the "Conciliar process for Justice, Peace and the Integrity of Creation"—this she followed up with a passion, as she was convinced that it is this process that brought grassroots action groups and church leadership into contact and thus established that justice issues have an ecclesial dimension. Her second major area of engagement was the "Program to Overcome Violence"; she even wrote her first book in English on this program.[36] She was also an important voice in the conduct of the Decade of the Churches in Solidarity with Women (1988-1998). A principled and deeply committed ecumenist, I refer to her once again in the last chapter of this book. She shared in her response, her confidence in women in the ecumenical movement.

> There have always been strong relationships among women in the ecumenical movement. We supported one another even when structures did divide. We need this voice. And as the impact has been so enormous since 1948, I hope and expect that there will be new strength. Women did have and will have a decisive impact on the ecumenical movement, I am sure.[37]

She summed up her prayer for the WCC:

> May it (the WCC) be a prophetic voice again over against all
> consensus desires. May there be courage to confront the pow-
> ers of violence and injustice. And may it be a platform for
> Christians to meet and share across the boundaries of culture,
> nationalism, capitalism and racism that are still so dominant
> today.[38]

Marie Assaad,[39] (1922-2018), a Coptic Orthodox lay woman
from Egypt, became the first woman appointed as the Deputy
General Secretary of the WCC in 1980—a position she retired
from in 1986. She went back to Cairo to continue her work
with rag-pickers and in training women in recycling waste to
produce hand-made paper. She passed away at the age of 96 on
September 2, 2018. As a pioneer in her leadership role in the
WCC, she did face occasional difficulties. Her diminutive fig-
ure gave male colleagues and church leaders cause to bypass her
leadership role when she was part of high-level delegations. But
her cheerful smile and pleasant disposition always won the day—
she was respected and honored by all. Her rich experience with
the Egyptian and World YWCAs, and in her own church as
well as projects with the marginalized, made her contributions
to the ecumenical movement stand out. Her comments on the
WCC are telling:

> Meeting women from across the world taught me how to the-
> ologize, how to accept differences and how to work for justice
> and peace. Yes, we need the WCC now more than ever be-
> fore. We need loyal people who are passionate to work across
> barriers of religion, race and ideologies for peace and justice.
> Even before I was part of the WCC, I was already involved in
> the ecumenical movement through the YWCA. But it was the
> WCC that taught me how to cope with heads of churches and
> develop the skills to make them listen to and respect women.[40]

Lois Wilson[41] was the first woman Moderator of the United
Church of Canada. A United Church minister, she represented
her church in the Central Committee and Executive Committee
of the WCC and was its North American President from 1983
to 1991. She played a key role in raising the profile of women
in the work of the WCC. She left her imprint on the WCC
because of her courage and outspokenness in the face of any injustice, especially when she saw that the leadership of women

was in anyway undermined. She is best known for her defense of human rights around the world with a specific passion for the re-unification of North and South Korea. She writes,

> The WCC is still a source of hope for many women—as it raises questions for the male "heads of churches" and the male dominated structures themselves. However, it would have helped if there could have been some process for reviewing staff appointments to ensure female appointments. It is really left to the whim of people in positions of power. Some method must be set in place for ensuring member churches nominate able female candidates for positions—and then follow the process to assess what happens! I think the WCC is the only hope for many women caught in male structures "at home." It may seem miniscule, but for many women, they found new life in the Ecumenical Decade of the Churches in Solidarity with Women, in feminist theology consultations, and in solidarity.[42]

Eleni Kasselouri Hatzivassiliadi,[43] a Greek Orthodox theologian who works in Thessaloniki, Greece, is recognized for her passion to bring women across the ecumenical movement into dialogue. She has played a key role in ensuring that Orthodox Christian women play a constructive and active role in the WCC's work, on their own terms. She is firm in her conviction that the ecumenical movement and the WCC can make a change in the lives of women and she therefore was always willing to work with Orthodox women and with women of all traditions to uphold the leadership and contributions of women. She had this to say:

> I can see hope and a creative role for the WCC mainly on the level of empowering the relationships among different Christian traditions and why not with other faiths, by creating safe spaces for dialogue and exchange of ideas. There is an urgent need for more meetings on education and formation of Christian identity, where of course new people should participate and be involved. I must confess that until now, many of the results, the proposals and the conclusions of the meetings and the official discussions that took place through or by the WCC are not well known and familiar to the grassroots and the local communities of my context. Although on the theological level, there are many articles, publications and other initiatives to inform people on these issues, many them still have hesitation on the necessity of ecumenical dialogue.[44]

Pauline Webb,[45] a Methodist from the UK, was the first lay woman to preach at an opening worship of an Assembly—the Sixth Assembly of the WCC in 1983, in Vancouver. She was born on June 28, 1927 and died on April 27, 2017 when she was eighty nine years old. She is best known as a relentless activist against racism, especially against the apartheid movement in South Africa. She was vice moderator of the WCC when the difficult decision was taken by the WCC to support the African National Congress and its political role in overthrowing the apartheid regime. Being with her in the ecumenical delegation that visited South Africa in 1991, and sharing with her the joy and privilege of visiting Nelson Mandela and Winnie Mandela in their home in Soweto was special. Her uninhibited joy in being in a "free" South Africa and in the presence of Nelson Mandela himself was infectious and compelling. Her contribution to the WCC will live on throughout its history.

In response to the questions I had asked her about the WCC, she wrote,

> I was the first woman to preach at a WCC Assembly (the Sixth Assembly of the WCC in Vancouver in 1983), despite the fact of not being ordained. Perhaps I was regarded as less of a threat that way! So, overall, though I once thought that women are at a great disadvantage in all spheres of life other than the home, I rejoice that I have lived to see far more doors of opportunity open to me and I hope more women will have the courage to take up the responsibilities of leadership and will be supported by other women as well as by men.

> A recent experience that gave me much satisfaction was when I was asked in 2009 to preach at an Ordination Service at the Methodist Conference, where the majority of ordinands are now women. This would have been quite impossible forty five years ago, at the time when I was campaigning for the ordination of women in my church and had to face fierce debates in our conference where our opponents ridiculed our ideas. I gave up any idea of ordination for myself but devoted a lot of time and energy to trying to persuade the conference to take us seriously. We were told we were being a threat to the unity of the Church. So, it has been a great satisfaction to me to see women being ordained now in all the major Protestant denominations in Britain. I note how the laughter has changed sides. Some of those who once ridiculed us are now themselves

ridiculed for failing to realize that clearly God is calling women into priesthood in all the churches today. I believe the Holy Spirit has much greater wisdom than the boasted wisdom of reactionary men![46]

Janice Love[47] from the United Methodist Church in the US has left an indelible mark on the WCC and continues to be a strong advocate for women and for the ecumenical movement. Her passionate commitment to the role of women saw her stand solidly with women in many a discussion. She was twenty three at the time she came to the Fifth Assembly of the WCC in Nairobi in 1975, a fresh graduate, and yet made a mark even as a youth participant and was one of the few youth delegates invited to serve on the prestigious Program Guidelines committee of the Assembly. She was a candidate for the Central Committee due to pressure from the youth and her church named her as their representative. She was re-elected for a second term and was in the Executive Committee. From that Assembly on, there was no turning back—she has served as moderator of the Public Issues Committee and several other important committees and has steered with efficiency and grace several sensitive discussions on the WCC. Her keen sense of justice and her deeply respectful stance has given her the needed skills to ensure that the WCC stayed on course in dealing with issues on a variety of special emphases of the Council.

Among the many roles she played, when she held office in the WCC, what will be most remembered will be her contributions to the dialogue between the Protestant and Orthodox churches. With conviction, courage and clarity, she steered many a discussion and decision making process in challenging the churches to stay together in dialogue and mutual commitment to ecumenical relationships. She rightfully claims that she demonstrated in her time her own role as being "undeniably competent, smart, savvy, reliable, and politically astute female leadership across three decades from the age of twenty-three, thus exercising substantial influence on the governance of the entire organization."[48] Reference is made to this contribution in a later chapter of this book.

THE STORY CONTINUES

The women in this book are just a few examples of the thousands of women in each place and all places that have had an impact on the ecumenical movement since its inception and till the present day—it is women, their stories, their lives, their visions that have driven the ecumenical movement and shaped it. But then, their voices, their struggles also indicate that they do not always feel included, some women would say that we have made but a small scratch, and some just give up in despair as their attempts to provide alternative models of inclusion and leadership do not go down well in the churches and in ecumenical structures which are deeply entrenched in patriarchy and the culture within which they have been formed, set up, organized and defined. In the last chapter of this book, I will explore this further.

Behind the work of the staff at the secretariat is the unstinting commitment and support of women, and some outstanding men, in the churches and in the WCC's governing bodies who worked together to initiate programs and supported proposals that came on the agenda for official approval. There were moments when funding was an issue, yet they stayed on track to see the work through.

The impact has been reciprocal—the churches and more specifically women in the churches have also been strongly influenced by the work of the WCC and the ecumenical movement and have looked to these institutions for inspiration and sometimes direction. Mary Grey, the British feminist theologian, writes, "The work of the WCC stimulated much attention to the position of women in church and society. From its conception there had been gender awareness."[49] The impact of its sixty odd year history on the life of women in general and more specifically on women in the churches and their theological work has never been studied in detail but references are made by women to its impact—this speaks more than statistics and figures could. Ursula King, for example, writes,

> The diffusion of feminist thinking across different cultures in association with the work of many Christian churches clearly demonstrates the profoundly ambivalent double dynamic of religion as both an oppressive force in people's lives, and a

liberating one. On the one hand, women are still being oppressed by patriarchal religious institutions. On the other hand,
these very institutions at a different level, help to bring about
the transformation of women's lives and thought, which in
turn cannot but lead to fundamental changes within these institutions themselves.

Examples of such active initiatives among women, of the
art of midwifery or bringing to birth, can be found among
others in the work of the World YWCA; the World Student
Christian Federation (WSCF); and especially the World
Council of Churches (WCC). The last plays a particularly active role.[50]

She goes on to describe some of the programs of the WCC
and their impact on women and the churches. She writes with
reference to women from the Global South.

The WCC has acted as an enabler for women: it has provided a
supportive network, financial and human resources, and many
opportunities through workshops, conferences, publications,
and places of study—all of which have helped the theological
development of women in different countries.[51]

From another part of the world, in an article appropriately
headed, "The Ecumenical Movement Awakening Women,"
Mavis Rose affirms that,

in view of the vitality and strength of the Women's Department
within the WCC, it was not surprising that the Australian
Council of Churches (ACC) should be active in efforts to raise
the status of Australian Christian women.[52]

In Australia, a Christian feminist group called Christian
Women Concerned was formed and a journal *Magdalene* was
published. The Australian Council of Churches also established
a Commission on the Status of Women, and from it the first
Anglican women's activist group called Anglican Women
Concerned, was born. The women in Australia were inspired
by the challenge issued by Bärbel Wartenberg-Potter, the then
Director of the Women's Program, at the 1983 Pre-Assembly
Women's event in Vancouver, that had spurred them on to ac-
tion. Wartenberg-Potter had asked,

Will the women delegates raise their voices on behalf of their
sisters at home and elsewhere? Will they dare to speak up in

the presence of their powerful church leaders? Will women support each-other or will they allow other loyalties to prevail: confessional, regional, national, racial, cultural? Will women refuse to build solidarity among them in order to avoid the accusations of dividing the community?[53]

These few reminders of the impact of the WCC's work on women in churches and the ecumenical movement are worth keeping squarely in mind.

The consideration of what some women in the ecumenical movement have to say, affirms the diversity of women who have had an influence on the ecumenical movement. This book will take a critical look at the history of women, to move to a new future for the ecumenical movement; and for women in the churches and in society. It does so with a vision.

ENDNOTES

[1] Anna Karin Hammar, "After Forty Years—Churches in Solidarity with Women?" *The Ecumenical Review* 40, nos. 3–4, (1988): 538. Anna Karin Hammar, a Lutheran ordained priest of the Church of Sweden, was Director of the WCC Women's Program from 1986-1990. She gave leadership to the designing and launch of the Ecumenical Decade of the Churches in Solidarity with Women, 1988-1998.

[2] Susannah Herzel, *A Voice for Women: The Women's Department of the World Council of Churches* (Geneva: World Council of Churches, 1981), ix.

[3] Lusmarina Campos Garcia, ordained Lutheran from Brazil in her sermon at the Easter Morning Service at the Evangelical Lutheran Church, Geneva, Switzerland, 2009. As noted down by the author.

[4] Pseudonyms used for Maria and Teresa for security reasons.

[5] An ecumenical team from different parts of the world was in Palestine on a Living Letters' pastoral visit organized in the context of the Decade to Overcome Violence (2001-2010) of the World Council of Churches.

[6] Purim is a festival that commemorates the deliverance of the Jewish people of the ancient Persian Empire from Haman's plot to annihilate them. This incident is recorded in the Book of Esther in the Bible. According to the story, Haman cast lots to determine the day upon which to exterminate the Jews—it is therefore a day of great importance to the Jewish people.

[7] In the year 1948, the state of Israel was founded, and the British Mandate came to an end. That same year, 750,000-900,000 Palestinians were displaced or expelled from their lands and the Jews began their settlements. Despite UN Resolution 194 granting the right of return for Palestinians in 1949, many today are still waiting to return home. The fighting came to an end in 1949 as armistice agreements were made and a "Green Line" separated the two parts of the land.

[8] Sheena Duncan, "Some Reflections on Rustenberg," in *Women Hold up Half the Sky: Women in the Church in Southern Africa*, eds. Ackerman, Draper and Mashinini (Pietermaritzburg: Cluster Publications, 1991), 386. Duncan, one of the two speakers at this conference, was for many years President of the Black Sash Movement, an anti-apartheid movement of white South Africans. She died in May 2010, aged seventy-seven.

[9] Pauline Webb headed religious broadcasting for the BBC (1979-1987) and was the first woman Vice Moderator of the Central Committee of the WCC (1968-1975).

[10] Duncan, "Some Reflections on Rustenberg," 386.

[11] From a transcript of the tape recording of the events of that evening as referred to in an unpublished article on "Another Perspective of Rustenburg: Words from Women," Marylee M. James, School of Theology, University of Natal, Pietermaritzburg (Unpublished manuscript, sent by email in September 1991 to the author).

[12] "Another Perspective of Rustenburg: Words from Women," 1991.

[13] http://www.womensnet.org.za/news/south-africas-other-epidemic-violence-against-women, accessed November 18, 2017.

[14] Micheline Kamba in a piece she wrote for this book. She wished to write it in English, a language she has received special training for, supported by the WCC. Her words are only slightly edited. Email message to author, December 5, 2009.

[15] Kamba, December 5, 2009.

[16] Central Committee of the World Council of Churches, "Statement on Sexual Violence against Women in the Democratic Republic of Congo," September 2, 2009, Geneva, accessed April 15, 2019, https://www.oikoumene.org/en/resources/documents/central-committee/2009/report-on-public-issues/statement-on-sexual-violence-against-women-in-the-democratic-republic-of-congo.

[17] Konds are an indigenous people's community who live in Central India. Deomali Adivasi Mahila Sangh is their organization (Deomali translates as "abode of the Gods"; Adivasi or first nations or indigenous peoples, Mahila which stands for women; and Sangh for Organization). This is the women's organization of indigenous peoples in that region of India. For a full account see Aruna Gnanadason, *Listen to the Women! Listen to the Earth!* (Geneva: WCC Publications, 2005).

[18] In discussion with Narango in her village in June, 2005. Our conversation was interpreted by Sasi Prabha who was then working with this community for over a decade. They had been protesting the take-over of their lands by the Indian government and others with economic interests.

31

[19] In discussion with Narango in her village as recorded by the author.

[20] In discussion with Narango.

[21] In discussion with Narango.

[22] Maria Mies and Vandana Shiva, *Ecofeminism* (Delhi: Kali for Women, 1993), 17.

[23] Amar Kumar Singh and C. Rajyalakshmi, "Status of Tribal Women in India" (Paper, National Workshop on the Status of Women organized by the Council for Social Development, New Delhi and sponsored by the National Commission of Women, New Delhi, 22-23 December 1993), accessed June 15, 2003, http://www.hsph.harvard.edu/Organizations.

[24] Afro-Brazilian Women and the Fight for Gender Inclusion, February 2, 2017, https://www.aaihs.org/afro-brazilian-feminists-and-the-fight-for-racial-and-gender-inclusion/

[25] Marilia Schuller, email message to the author on December 31, 2009 in response to the question, "How had the World Council of Churches influenced you and your ongoing work?"

[26] Annathaie Abhayasekara had served on the Advisory Group of the Program to Combat Racism from 1975-1983. Her first encounter with the WCC was as a Youth participant at the Fourth Assembly of the WCC in Uppsala in 1968. She also served on the WCC Central Committee and its Executive Committee from 1983 till 1991. In discussion with the author in Hatton, Sri Lanka, May 2010.

[27] In this last section of this chapter, I have included brief comments that a small group of selected women make regarding their hopes for the ecumenical movement—these were all through email exchanges.

[28] Bärbel Wartenberg Potter, a Lutheran theologian from Germany, retired as a Bishop of the region of Holstein Lübeck (2001-2008). She was Director of the then Sub-Unit on Women 1980-85.

[29] Bärbel Wartenberg-Potter, e-mail message to author, January 7, 2010.

[30] Mercy Amba Oduyoye, a Methodist theologian from Ghana, ended her work with the WCC as Deputy General Secretary in 1994.

[31] Mercy Amba Oduyoye, email message to author, December 17, 2009.

[32] Agnes Aboum, presently Moderator of the WCC's Central Committee. She is also the executive director of the organization, TAABCO Research and Development Consultants in Kenya, which was established in 1997 and offers consultancy work for civil society organizations and aid organizations. In 2017, she was awarded the Lambeth Cross for Ecumenism by the Archbishop of Canterbury "for her exceptional contribution to the Ecumenical Movement, for her work with the World Council of Churches and currently as its Moderator."

[33] Alternatives to Globalization Addressing People and Earth (AGAPE 1997-1998) initiated by the Justice, Peace, Creation Team of the WCC became controversial as it exposed once again, the divide on perceptions of the role of the churches in global concerns, between churches from the Global North and the Global South. Accessed September 2017. https://www.oikoumene.org/en/resources/documents/

assembly/2006-porto-alegre/3-preparatory-and-background-documents/
alternative-globalization-addressing-people-and-earth-agape

[34] Agnes Aboum, e-mail message to author, September 3, 2010.

[35] Margot Käßmann, a Lutheran theologian from Germany was Landesbischöfin of the Evangelical-Lutheran Church of Hanover in Germany and still serves as a pastor of the church. On October 28, 2009, she was elected to lead the Evangelical Church in Germany, a federation of Protestant church bodies in Germany an office from which she stepped down on February 24, 2010.

[36] Margot Käßmann, *Overcoming Violence: The Challenge to the Churches in All Places* (Geneva: WCC Publications, 1998).

[37] Margot Käßmann, e-mail message to author, September 4, 2009, and February 16, 2018.

[38] Margot Käßmann, e-mail message to author, 2009, 2018.

[39] Marie Assaad, a Coptic Orthodox lay woman from Egypt, was a member of her local YWCA in Cairo and in 1947 represented the movement at the second World Conference of Christian Youth in Oslo. Marie then went on to work at the World Office of the YWCA in Geneva as Program Assistant in the Youth Department from 1952 to 1953. In 1980, she became the first woman appointed to the executive structures of the World Council of Churches, as the first female Deputy General Secretary and retired from that position in 1986.

[40] Marie Assaad, e-mail message to author, September 15, 2009.

[41] Lois Wilson was the first woman Moderator of the United Church of Canada, from 1980 to 1982, and North American President of the WCC for a term (1983-1991).

[42] Lois Wilson, in personal correspondence, September 12, 2009.

[43] Eleni Kasselouri Hatzivassiliadi is a New Testament scholar from the Greek Orthodox Church and teaches "Studies in Orthodox Theology" at the master's program of the Hellenic Open University in Thessaloniki. She had previously worked with the Volos Academy for Theological Studies among other things. She was vice-president of the European Society of Women in Theological Research (1999-2001) and served on the Steering Group of the WCC Women's Program's "Women's Voices and Visions on Being Church" project (2002-2006).

[44] Eleni Kasselouri Hatzivassiliadi, e-mail message to the author, January 15, 2010.

[45] Pauline Webb, a Methodist from the United Kingdom, was Vice-Moderator of the World Council of Churches (1968-1975). She was organizer of Religious Broadcasting in the BBC's World Service (1979-1987).

[46] Pauline Webb in personal correspondence, December 3, 2009.

[47] Janice Love's active engagement with the WCC began in 1975 when she came as a youth delegate of her church at the Fifth Assembly of the World Council of Churches, in Nairobi, Kenya. In 1995, she headed the WCC delegation to the Fourth World Conference on Women in Beijing.

[48] Janice Love in personal correspondence, December 2009; March 2018.

[49] Mary C. Grey, "Feminist Theologies, European," in *Dictionary of Feminist Theologies*, eds. Letty Russell and Shannon Clarkson (Louisville, Kentucky: Westminster John Knox Press, 1986), 103.

[50] Ursula King, ed., *Feminist Theologies from the Third World: A Reader* (London: SPCK and Maryknoll, New York: Orbis Books, 1994), 8.

[51] King, *Feminist Theologies from the Third World: A Reader*, 11.

[52] Mavis Rose, "The Ecumenical Movement Awakening Women," Freedom from Sanctified Sexism—Women Transforming the Church (Queensland, Australia: Allira Publications, 1996), 111.

[53] Bärbel Wartenberg-Potter quoted by Mavis Rose, "The Ecumenical Movement Awakening Women," 113.

CHAPTER 2

WOMEN HAVE MADE A DIFFERENCE

We will become a new and living community in Christ, a
growing stream of resurrection people, a people of God on
a faith journey of hope. We will be filled with the inevitable
fears and doubts caused by the stones we will encounter on the
way, but we will move on compelled by love. We will find the
challenge of the risen Savior. "Do not be amazed; you seek Jesus
of Nazareth, who was crucified. He has risen; he is not here . . .
but go, tell his disciples . . . ."

Easter Message 1988[1]

Women all over the world have served their churches faithfully
and have time and again acted as the conscience of the Christian
community as they work for justice and peace in their societies, in the world, between nations, and in their churches and
in the ecumenical movement. Women's voices have in the past
decades, become sharper, more courageous and compassionate
and they have established a space for themselves in ecumenical
dialogue even if their visibility in numbers is not always reflec-
tive of their capabilities and commitment to contribute. This
chapter opens with remembering and celebrating some historic moments and programs in the work of the WCC related to
women, not so much as a historical record, but more to honor
the women who have made it all happen and to highlight the
range of concerns that women have brought onto the agenda of
the ecumenical movement and to their churches. An "impact assessment of the WCC's programs related to women" is not easy
as it has been so indirect and profound—it cannot be numerical-
ly accounted for—this book makes a small contribution to the
assessment of the WCC's work.

SOME GLIMPSES OF EVENTS AND PROGRAMS

Ecumenical work among women began much before the WCC was established. It began when, in the last decades of the nineteenth century, women came together to form the Young Women's Christian Association in England, which by the beginning of the twentieth century became a global movement of women. The World Young Women's Christian Association (WYWCA) has since had its headquarters in Geneva, and "With its pioneering history of uniting women of different churches and races in a world membership movement. . . . (WYWCA) had much to contribute to the nascent ecumenical movement."[2]

Twila Cavert was a member of the YWCA from the United States of America and had accompanied her husband to Geneva who was there for discussions with a small group of church leaders from largely Europe and North America to discuss the formation of a new world ecumenical body, later to be called the World Council of Churches. Twila, who was invited to be part of this important meeting, took this as an opportunity to visit the YWCA international offices. Here, the women decided that the proposed WYWCA study on the status and role of women in the church initiated by them was wrongly placed. In Cavert's words, "Frankly, I don't think the World YWCA is the place where this business about women in the church should be dealt with. I think the World Council of Churches ought to get busy on it."[3] The women invited the church leaders who were at the meeting of the WCC in-formation, to discuss with them the future of the study on the status and role of women to encourage them to make it a church focused and led project. The leaders saw the logic of what was being proposed and thus for a period of two and a half years, a group of women were requested to organize the study. Questionnaires were prepared, translated and distributed widely to the churches and women's networks, and the responses were collated and finalized as a report to be presented to the churches.

To plan for women's participation at the First Assembly, Twila Cavert made links with Kathleen Bliss and (Mrs.) Geoffrey Bishop *(sic.)* of England, as well as Suzanne de Diétrich and Madeleine Barot of France. A pre-assembly meeting of women was planned and held at Baarn, near Amsterdam in 1948.

The Baarn report was then presented to the First Assembly of the World Council of Churches by Sarah Chakko, a Syrian Orthodox woman from India. The Report includes responses from fifty-eight countries, each fifty to one hundred pages in length. The report acknowledges the cooperation received from some of the older churches "whose constant awareness and tradition lead us back through the centuries to the priceless early days of the Christian church."[4]

One can only be amazed at the courage and persistence of these our fore-mothers, for preparing the way for the participation of future generations of women in the ecumenical movement and the WCC. From those origins, the movement of women in the ecumenical movement grew—each period adding its own color and vibrancy with its own character, programs and distinctive strategies. Looking back, Pauline Webb writes,

> There seems always to have been a fear that too much activity on the part of women would rock the ecumenical boat. Boats always are rocked by a wind, and maybe it is the wind of the Spirit that has impelled women to go on making their presence felt with increasing force during the second half of the twentieth century.[5]

In 1949, the World Council of Churches, Central Committee meeting in Chichester, England, set up an official Commission on the Life and Work of Women in the Church with Sarah Chakko as chair and Kathleen Bliss as secretary. Visser't Hooft, the first General Secretary of the WCC, commented on its work:

> The significance of this Commission must be regarded in the light of the ecumenical movement, which seeks to restore the wholeness of the churches, and to work for its renewal. Unless women are given more responsibility in the life of local churches, that renewal cannot be achieved.[6]

The Evanston Assembly in 1954 accepted that the Commission be converted into a department of the WCC and under the leadership of Madeline Barot, from France the Department on the Cooperation of Men and Women in Church and Society was born. The going was certainly not easy, and it had to be repeatedly asserted that this was not a program to "speak about women's rights."[7] The diversity of positions on issues such as the ordination of women and birth control caused tensions in the nascent department. Madeleine Barot ensured that attention was directed to cooperation between women and men not only in the church, but also in society, a commitment which has been sustained over the decades. She made the best use of the fact that the WCC secretariat situated in Geneva opened up possibilities for Christian women to participate in United Nations (UN) instruments such as the World Health Organization (WHO) and the International Labor Office (ILO). The WCC has continued to keep these connections (later being entitled to "observer status" at the UN); and has contributed to the global movements of women. The WCC facilitated a delegation to the Third World Conference on Women held in Nairobi in 1985; and took a delegation of fifty women to the NGO Forum related to the Fourth World Conference in Beijing in 1995, with Janice Love from the United Methodist Church, USA, heading the four-member delegation to the official inter-governmental conference. Since then, the WCC has had a delegation of women attending annual meetings of the UN's Commission on the Status of Women (CSW) in New York; and has actively engaged in the network of Christian women who have formed themselves into Ecumenical Women United running alongside the CSW, to strategize as women religious in UN processes.

To go back to the work of the WCC, after the Third WCC Assembly in New Delhi, 1961, the women's program responded to the needs expressed there by including the concern for family, marriage and problems in relationships, as well as widowhood, and the plight of single women and divorced women into its work. The discussions at the Fourth Assembly in Uppsala, 1968, inspired a shift in the focus of the work and a new organization of the work. Concerns of sexism, racism and poverty, as well as the need for legal reforms to safeguard the rights of women became part of the agenda of the WCC. Under the leadership of Brigalia Bam from South Africa who headed the newly formed women's desk in the new structure of the WCC, justice for women in church and society gained ascendancy in the programming.

Living in exile because of her own engagement in the anti-apartheid movement, Brigalia Bam brought with her the impact of political freedom struggles in her own country and in many other countries in the Global South. There was also the influence of the newly emerging women's liberation movements all over the world. Brigalia prioritized leadership training of women and stressed on the importance for women to articulate their own distinctive approaches to theology, born out of their everyday experiences. "Given Brigalia Bam's South African background and the growing feminist movement, the language, tactics, pressures, and concerns of politics ran right through the women's desk's work in the 1970s."[8]

Sexism in the Seventies (Berlin, 1974) was a pathbreaking global conference organized by the WCC in this period. It will be remembered as Brigalia Bam's gift to the ecumenical movement. Pauline Webb, the then Vice Moderator of the WCC's Central Committee, who chaired the world conference, writes with tongue-in-cheek: "Sexism was a new word coming into the ecumenical vocabulary and many ribald comments were made about it at the time. Some even suggested that we had planned a conference on sexual activity in old age!"[9] This major consultation, was to change the face of the work, and prepared the WCC and the women in the churches for the UN's International Women's Year (1975) as well as for the WCC's Fifth Assembly in Nairobi—both of which were held in 1975. Sexism was certainly a new word for WCC and denoted a shift in thinking in the women's program. The church, it implied, will be unable to reflect a true community of women and men until it manages to resolve questions of structure and power which underpin the male-dominated order in society and in the church. It was decided by the organizers that Berlin would be an all-women consultation, and this was the pattern maintained through the 1970s.

SEXISM—A VIRULENT HERESY ANALOGOUS TO RACISM[10]

The Berlin conference was not just another conference—it made a difference to the role and status of women in the ecumenical movement and in the churches. In introducing the report of the conference, Pauline Webb writes:

> It is not just a matter of acknowledging the physical difference between men and women. . . . It is rather recognizing that alongside this difference there have been different histories, different expectations, and a different sense of identity, and

39

an association with the structures of power that have created a male order in almost all human society and certainly within the Church, making it impossible for the Church to foreshadow the truly human community. So, it is for the sake of that community that we Christian women come now to examine the heresy of sexism and to explore ways to overcoming it that will liberate both men and women for a new partnership in the gospel.[11]

Far reaching recommendations, covering a depth of concerns were developed through working groups on theology; strategies and structures; partnership; women in politics; women in economic structures; and education. The tenor of this gathering becomes clear by the affirmation of liberation theology "as one method to help us express our faith out of our own particular experiences."[12] The conference called for the encouragement of the churches and the WCC to enable women to study theology, by setting aside scholarships for women. The Berlin conference also spoke about sexist language and imagery and urged the WCC to provide guidelines for inclusive language and to "correct sexist errors in future translations" of the Bible.[13] The working groups even addressed the issue of looking at partnership as more than marriage between a woman and a man and to affirm the right of individuals to live alternative lifestyles for "persons of variant sexual orientations."[14]

Additionally, the working groups stressed the need for the churches to develop strategies to work on their prophetic mission by engaging with people's struggles for justice and peace; for human rights and the liberation of women. The conference addressed racism and colonialism as well as justice in international trade and in the international monetary system. The concern about the exploitation of poorer nations in trade, nuclear expansion and in the arms industry was also addressed.[15] The conference called on the churches to endorse and make their own plans for marking the UN's International Year for Women 1975, by developing policies to ensure participation of women in decision making bodies of the church; and to make marriage liturgies more just in commitments to reciprocity between women and men. It also encouraged the churches to promote the World Population Year as an opportunity to ensure that family planning programs are just and cover the rights of women.

I have quoted extensively from this report to underline that women in the ecumenical movement have always been at the forefront of naming and challenging difficult issues. This conference did much to change the focus and direction of the work responding directly to the lives and struggles of women in all societies.

THE COMMUNITY OF WOMEN AND MEN IN THE CHURCH—AN UNPRECEDENTED CONGREGATION-BASED STUDY PROCESS

In 1975, at the Fifth Assembly in Nairobi, the report of the World Conference on Sexism in the '70s: Discrimination against Women (Berlin, 1974) was received and the Assembly recommended "the just participation of women in the political, economic, ecclesial areas of life and in the decision making bodies of the WCC."[16] Additionally,

> The call was made for a thorough examination of the theological assumptions concerning women and men in church and society and for a process of reflection which would enable men and women to find their identity in relationships with one another.[17]

Consequently, in 1976, a major congregation-based study process on the Community of Women and Men was launched as a joint project of the WCC's Faith and Order Commission with the then Sub-unit on Women. The study was to consider the fresh theological insights emerging from the women's movements and reflect on their implications for the wider church. Under the leadership of Constance Parvey, a Lutheran feminist theologian from the US, the study focused on three sets of questions: personal and cultural; church teachings; and church structures. Theological study groups were organized in many parts of the world to bring the voices of all women into the discussion. This brought local congregations, more than ever before and in most places for the first time, into a reflection on the biblical, anthropological and theological roots of the relationship between women and men. The method of the Community Study was interdisciplinary, being co-sponsored by the Faith and Order Commission and the Women's program.

41

As Melanie May, a long-time member of the Faith and Order Commission, writes, "In this way the study made clear that the search for the unity of the church cannot be undertaken without attention to the realities of the world in which the church lives and to which it witnesses."[18]

The Community Study presented new perspectives on issues of identity, sexuality, marriage, family life, Scripture and tradition in relation to the community of women and men, theological education, worship and ministry, including ordained ministry. Melanie describes how this process had drawn on a "local experience-based methodology" to influence global challenges to the ecumenical movement.[19]

The emphasis was on the "integral connection of the search for church unity and the healing of the human community."[20] It called for a renewed church. The methodology of the Community Study had its impact on the work of the Faith and Order Commission so much so that the Faith and Order study on "Church and World: The Unity and the Renewal of Human Community"[21] has a chapter titled, "Unity and Renewal and the Community of Women and Men." This chapter describes how, ". . . the community of women and men in both church and society is still marred by evident injustices from which the church struggles to emerge."[22] It also speaks of the role of theological anthropology and of the importance of unraveling some of its impact on the way the roles of women and men in community are perceived.

> As prophetic sign, the church participates in God's reconciling will for humanity and is thus called to show forth, in its own life, how one of the most profound and pervasive divisions within creation—that between male and female—may be overcome in the common belonging of men and women "in Christ."[23]

Constance Parvey describes, with warmth, what was at the heart of the Community Study process. She writes: "Perhaps the most valuable part of the study has been the friendships and new models of working together at every level that the program generated."[24] This largest ever congregation and locally based Study process initiated by the WCC, ensured participation at all levels. The perfect collaboration between the Faith and Order movement and the Women in Church and Society program of the WCC has never been replicated again between these two programs. The Community Study came to conclusion at a world conference held in Sheffield, UK, in 1981 when the findings of the Study process were discussed.

In the work on women, over the past sixty years or so, one can observe a flow—one program inspires another, pushing the churches forward to new areas in their commitments to women. In Sheffield, when more than 200 women and men came together, the women from the Global South present there called for an opportunity to voice some of their concerns on the floor of the conference as they felt that the Study did not respond to their contextual human concerns. Their voice was received with mixed reactions, some supporting the women from the Global South, others claiming that it was "a brief flare up and has died a quick and proper death."[25] The Sheffield Report does acknowledge that of the 200 odd responses received to the study booklet on the Community of Women and Men that had been sent out by the WCC, 80 percent were from local groups in North America and Europe which "might have been an indication that the questions in this study may not have the urgency and priority for other areas."[26]

The women from the Global South did acknowledge in their statement that the study had brought an awakening of sexism in their churches, but they ask for recognition of the web of oppression of racism, classism and sexism that engulfs their lives. Their contention was that wholeness and community within the church can be realized only in the context of the larger struggle for human wholeness.

The concern the women raised in Sheffield was reflected in future programming. The WCC established in 1994 the Women and Rural Development Fund to support "survival initiatives of women" by providing seed grants to them for small businesses to make themselves self-sufficient. Under the leadership of Priscilla Padolina from the Philippines, the fund supported hundreds of small survival initiatives of women over the years. It became an important instrument to build a network of women at the grassroots—for many years, the WCC's work with women was identified with the Fund in some parts of the world. Ranjini Rebera, from Sri Lanka, who documented the evaluation of the Fund describes it "as an attempt to deal with the inequalities within the global village that continue to treat women as a faceless component in the process of development."[27]

A few years later, challenges came, largely from African women, that the focus of the fund on "survival initiatives" for women through small grants implied that most women should be content with survival, while the minority of women with access to wealth and the resources of the earth can thrive. It was at that time that the All Africa Conference of Churches (AACC) launched a handbook and a training process on "economic literacy." This was designed and led by Omega Bula from Zambia, who was then Program Executive for women in the AACC. This process was followed through all over the African continent and enabled women in the villages and cities to understand why they live in poverty and the global forces that play into their lives. This initiative inspired the direction the Women and Rural Development Fund was to take. It was further developed, notably under the leadership of Thembisile Majola from South Africa, to include a longer-term reflection on the way the lives of women are impacted by the global economy and the development paradigm that undergirds it.

Thus, after the Fifth Assembly of the WCC in Harare in 1998, the work on women and economic justice was restructured to provide a feminist critique of economic structures; and to explore feminist alternatives. Women economists, ethicists, theologians and activists were brought into the WCC's ongoing work on seeking for alternatives to economic globalization and its impact on the earth—the AGAPE process as it was called. Athena Peralta, a feminist economist from the Philippines, was responsible for this work and through a series of discussion groups, regional conferences, dialogues and visits, women raised timely challenges to the WCC to take stock of the specific impact of the world economy on the lives of women. Some of the issues raised by women include the concern that economic globalization has not improved women's situation, contrarily, it has aggravated inequality between women and men, especially for women who live in the context of multiple oppressions of race, class, diverse ethnicities and caste identities. Maternal and child health, unhealthy and sometimes hazardous working conditions for women, sex segregation and the abuse of sexuality in the media industry, forms of discrimination in the labor market and the underpayment of women, livelihood losses in the agricultural sector, undervaluation of domestic care-giving workloads, increasing violence against women in work places and in the home are some of the issues identified in this process. Additionally, the process did identify alternatives calling for just and sustainable economic reforms to improve the quality of life of women. What was called a "care economy" was developed to encourage women and men to live in more caring and just relationships with each other and with the earth.[28] Thus, as a result of the discussion on Sexism in the '70s, the way was paved for a sea change in the direction and focus of the work done by the WCC.

GIVING VISIBILITY AND VOICE TO WOMEN

Going back to the discussion on the ways in which women have participated in the institutional life of the WCC, in 1981, the Central Committee of the WCC meeting in Dresden, Germany approved (after much debate) that "the principle of equal participation of women and men be a goal towards which we move, starting with the composition of the WCC decision making and consultative bodies during and after the Sixth Assembly."[29] This created the climate for the then Director of the Women's Sub-Unit, as the program was then called, Bärbel Wartenberg Potter, from Germany to systematically monitor, with her team all programs of the WCC to ensure women's voices and full participation. They worked diligently along with women in the governing bodies to make certain the visibility of women in all aspects of the life of the Sixth Assembly of the WCC in Vancouver (1983), which marked a turning point in the life of the WCC and its commitments to women. "Advocacy for women" was the watchword that guided all the work under the leadership of Bärbel Wartenberg-Potter. Official church delegates to the Assembly increased from 22 percent at the Nairobi Assembly to 30 percent at Vancouver. The visible and strong presence of women was evident as speakers in twelve of the plenary sessions; and with women as facilitators, as leaders in Bible Study, participating in worship and in other aspects of the

Assembly. For the first time ever a woman, Pauline Webb, was the preacher at the opening worship.

By the time of the Seventh Assembly of the WCC in Canberra, Australia, 1991, the Ecumenical Decade of the Churches in Solidarity was in full swing. It had been launched in 1988. It was at this Assembly that the Korean feminist theologian, Chung Hyun Kyung, made a powerful and moving multi-media presentation including the sound of traditional Korean drums and dancers; with aboriginal artists from the local context joining in, on the theme, "Come Holy Spirit, Renew the Whole Creation." Her presentation was challenging to traditional theologians who branded it as syncretistic; but as Pauline Webb describes it, "for all of us who were there at Canberra, the abiding image had become that of the woman holding in her hand a torch of fire, an appropriate symbol of that Spirit that has led God's faithful people through the centuries and had brought us that far on our ecumenical pilgrimage."[30] It was also this Assembly that had been marred by an incident of sexual violence—more on the WCC's response to this will be discussed in the chapter on violence against women.

THE ECUMENICAL DECADE OF THE CHURCHES IN SOLIDARITY WITH WOMEN—DID IT MAKE ITS MARK?

The 1987 WCC central committee in Geneva had given its approval for an Ecumenical Decade of the Churches in Solidarity with Women (1988-1998); an idea that emerged from the UN Decade on Women that had ended in 1985. When the report of the WCC's participation in the UN Decade was being presented, it was a Nigerian Methodist Bishop who suggested that the time was ripe for a Churches' Decade that could work more consistently on the challenges women were raising. Under the leadership of Anna Karin Hammar, a Lutheran theologian from Sweden who was then Director of the WCC's women's program, the Ecumenical Decade of the Churches in Solidarity with Women was launched. It was a Decade when the community of women and men in the churches would focus attention on women and their leadership and participation in church and society. At the heart of the Ecumenical Decade was the call to the churches to reflect on theological and ecclesiological structures that deny women their full participation and to plan strategic steps to bring changes. It was to empower women and affirm their leadership in church and society. Throughout the Decade, the active solidarity of men was sought.

I joined the staff of the WCC in 1991 and participated in a meeting of women from the regions, to reflect on where the Decade was in each region and the consensus was that there seemed to be a loss of focus—in some countries there was enthusiasm but not everywhere. Rather than being a decade of churches in solidarity with women, it was steadily becoming a decade of women in solidarity with women, or of women in solidarity with the churches. This was not viewed as a negative outcome of the Decade as there was much to celebrate in the increasing solidarity among women locally, nationally, regionally and globally, but it was underlined that there had been high expectations when the Decade had been launched. There was a yearning for more focused action from the churches in solidarity with women. There was also the hope that women's theologies and spirituality and their methodologies of solidarity and engagement would be embraced into the life of the churches. The women from the regions proposed ecumenical team visits to all member churches to "give the Decade back to the churches." Rather than organizing big regional gatherings of the churches for church leaders to encounter each other and share what they had achieved in their churches, this direct contact with each church in its own place would be a more effective way to assess how far the churches have moved in their commitments to women, it was decided.

An elaborate program of team visitations was set in motion with Nicole Fischer Duchable from Switzerland taking leadership. Some 75 ecumenically composed teams of two men and two women visited 300 churches as well as ecumenical initiatives in all regions of the world. The 1997 report of the ecumenical teams, entitled *Living Letters*, documents the determination and endurance of women to overcome the struggles they face which includes violence, the lack of participation in the life of the churches, racism and economic injustice. Women from many churches, in all regions, identified these as issues that plague them as they try to address them in a variety of ways. Some issues are addressed by women helping each other, and others have seen churches or women from churches working with secular organizations and women of other faiths to achieve their goals. The teams encountered the cultural, ecclesiastical and local realities of the churches and challenged churches wherever they could, to reflect on the need for structural change and transformation of their liturgical and ecclesial life to make them inclusive of women.

As Bertrice Wood of the United Church of Christ USA, the then vice-Moderator of the WCC's Advisory Group on Women described it:

> The "Living Letters" team visits pointed out that women are indeed the pillars of the church in all regions of the world. They are the marrow in the Body of Christ. Just as on that first Easter morning, the faithfulness and witness of women continues to sustain and nurture the church. We learned irrefutably that women love the church, as we always have. In our time, as the "Living Letters" discovered in visit after visit, women are, more than ever, recognizing their God-given gifts as invaluable contributions for the life of the whole church and the whole world. And women are clearly calling the church, as the Body of Christ, to embody Christ's ministry of justice wherever there is injustice, to embrace Christ's example of inclusivity wherever there are persons excluded, be it in the church or in society. . . Women, and thankfully many men, have not been sitting by idly. We learned how global, how ecumenical, is the commitment and the energy to overcome whatever are the obstacles which divide people in our churches and block our ability to live in solidarity with all persons in the world.[31]

Churches were encouraged to define the questions that are of greatest importance to them in their own context, but the following were proposed as possible areas for the churches' engagement with women. Violence against women in church and society; economic injustice and its impact on women; racism, casteism, rights of women from indigenous communities; and the participation of women in all aspects of the life and ministry of the churches—were the proposed focus areas. Just two of the issues addressed by the churches are discussed later in this book—the issue of ordination of women and that of violence against women.

THE DECADE'S IMPACT ON WOMEN, IN THEIR OWN WORDS

Women around the world had invested energy and commitment into the "success" of the Ecumenical Decade of the Churches in Solidarity with Women. The churches and the ecumenical movement too had done their share, by setting aside resources for this at the world level and in many individual churches and in nationally based ecumenical organizations of the churches, wherever they exist. The Decade concluded with a spectacular Festival held at the Belvedere Technical Teachers Training College in the suburbs of Harare, Zimbabwe, under the caring commitment and organizational acumen of the women of the member churches of the Zimbabwe Council of Churches led by two competent women leaders, Prisca Munanyara and Connie Mabusela. Some 1200 women including a select number of men met at the Festival to take stock of what had been achieved during the Decade and to discuss the challenges that remained. Women used that space to reflect on what they would do with their collective power. They sat at round tables with no hierarchy in the seating—women bishops sat with women in the pews, women evangelists with women theologians, and discussed their struggles and hopes.

Some comments culled out of the official press releases of the WCC during the Decade Festival reveal some of the successes of the Decade—symbolic of the impact that the WCC's programs have on the churches and on women. They also did point to the challenges that do remain:

"During the past ten years we were doing an awareness project. Now that the church is aware of the concerns of women, it is time to act to correct and to act to transform and this is a challenge that will take a long time," Mercy Oduyoye said. She went on to insist that it is time for the churches to implement all the recommendations that were made during the Decade. She challenged churches and church-related organizations to strengthen their women's desks so that the recommendations can be acted on. She boldly proclaimed that she saw no obstacle for women to participate fully in the ecumenical movement. "We have to work hard to get there, there is no rule that says women should not be in top leadership of the church," she said. "The sky is the limit.[32]

Musimbi Kanyoro, from Kenya, the then General Secretary of the World Young Women's Christian Association (WYWCA), who had earlier directed the Lutheran World Federation's Women in Church and Society Program, said the Decade was significant because women from all over the world were able to sit together and discuss issues that affect them in their diverse realities. At the Festival's opening worship service, Musimbi Kanyoro said,

> We as women can no longer just call for solidarity . . .but rather we need to be part of a redefining and redesigning process for all the changes we hoped for during this Decade. Even though we celebrate the end of the Decade, we must be sure not to accept being dismissed, but rather be ready to listen even more carefully and speak more articulately. We will not accept our gifts being minimized, but rather we will lift up all the gifts of the people of God.[33]

Talking about the future role of women in the church, Musimbi Kanyoro said she was happy that women in the ecumenical world were now empowering themselves theologically, through formal and informal training, and that women were also familiarizing themselves with the structures of the church. This, she said, was strengthening the position of women in the church. "Our strength is going to be visible to the church. We have been knocking silently on the doors of the church, but now we are not outside anymore."[34]

Many eminent women who gathered at the Festival in Harare have long memories of the struggle for equal status in church leadership. "The concept is that a mega-experience such as this is really the fusion of other related experiences," said Dr. Thelma Adair, a veteran woman leader from the Presbyterian Church in the US. She asked, "Can this flow from the past bring in new people and meld to move out into a new formation?"[35]

When Susan Karava Setae was chair of the Papua New Guinea Council of Churches' Women's Committee, she used the Decade as the platform to urge greater participation of women in leadership roles in the church. One campaign called on denominational leaders to place more women pastors in congregations. Ordination of women was already church policy, but graduating women seminarians were being assigned teaching and other jobs outside parish leadership. On one occasion in

Susan's church, the audience's response was an angry one. "The men shouted us down," she recalled. "When they said, 'women, wash your mouths.' We replied, 'men, wash your hearts.'"[36]

Susan Setae, a member of the Ecumenical Decade's global planning committee and a delegate to the Decade Festival in Harare, had served the women of Papua New Guinea for more than three decades. She is a trained teacher and lecturer, who moved early in life to become a community development activist. She cited gains for Papua New Guinea's church women. "A lot of churches have responded very well," she said. "During the Decade, we have more female clergy and an increasing number of women at ecumenical decision making meetings. More women are enrolling for theological education. And now a woman is General Secretary of the Pacific Conference of Churches." Concern for women's role and status in society also has been part of work in Papua New Guinea under the Ecumenical Decade umbrella. "Church and society aren't separable," said Setae, who challenges the church to be concerned about social issues and not be just preoccupied with its own administration.

In Papua New Guinea, domestic violence is a problem of great concern. Many women have no property rights, the life expectancy among women is just forty seven years, and the maternal mortality rate is high, said Susan Setae, herself a mother of four. "We have a very high illiteracy rate," she continued. "Sixty percent of our rural women cannot read or write. That's violence too." "Involvement in the Ecumenical Decade has built me as a person." But, she acknowledged the mixed results—along with the success, there has been a backlash. "The Decade has made me become more aware of the problems we have as women. The Decade has done a lot of good but at the same time some of us have been victims because we challenged the churches."[37]

NEXT STEPS ON THE JOURNEY WITH WOMEN

The delegation from Latin America to the Decade Festival came with the request that there be another Decade of the Churches in Solidarity with Women so that further work can be done—this was not possible or feasible. It was self-evident that women will face many challenges in what is to be a " 'decade less' future . . . we no longer have a Decade project to depend on, we cannot use it as a crutch. . . . we still have to create the spaces and keep up the energy to talk to the churches so as to keep their commitments alive. This, we need because there is yet much to be done."[38] And the concerns of the women had some truth to it. Decade related activities were stopped in many places—in the All Africa Conference of Churches, in Germany, in Canada . . . too many to name here. It was almost as if the churches were saying—we have done our bit, we will now move on to other priorities.

Gail Allan of the United Church in Canada participated in many Decade related activities both nationally and internationally and was also present at the end of Decade Festival. She wrote her doctoral thesis on the Decade and the Churches in Canada.[39] Her central thesis, in my understanding, is that the success of the Decade lay in the way it bridged women together in Canada and globally—solidarity among women was achieved. While analyzing some of the challenges in building such solidarity, she calls for "radical inclusiveness" of allowing what she terms "dangerous stories" to interrogate and reshape a community's self-definition.[40] She quotes Omega Bula who describes the solidarity of global sisterhood as "a way of life. . . . that resists oppression." Omega Bula found in the Decade (and in the UN's Beijing Conference on Women) the promise of "communities of hope" and "networks of resistance" cooperating in constructive action, but open to mutual critique and aware of power and class privilege. For Omega Bula, solidarity means both that "we find ways to celebrate our oneness as women of the world" and that "we take a clear stand to resist oppression, to struggle for justice, to challenge, inspire and motivate people into action on life issues."[41]

In summary, the Decade raised questions about the violence and exclusion that is a part of women's daily lives in many parts of the world. Stark realities of racism, economic injustice and violence which women experience have come to the open. But women have also spoken of their longing for the realization of a more authentic and faithful community of women and men in the church. The Decade demonstrated how women stood in solidarity with each other and of their commitment to a renewed

52

community of the church. The teams heard descriptions of ways in which something of a renewed community can be achieved, thanks to the impact of the Decade. Women often affirmed the diversity of their experiences and were aware of the multi-faith contexts in which they strive to be a community that respects plurality.

While this affirmation of the new expressions of solidarity among women is commendable, it only very partially fulfilled the expectations of what this Decade was to accomplish. Dame Mary Tanner, of the Church of England and former Moderator of the Faith and Order Commission, speaks of solidarity as being an integral responsibility of the church.

> The church has a special responsibility of attentive solidarity with the women of the world. It is not enough for women to be in solidarity with women. The whole church is called to a ministry of solidarity, with a bias toward women and children. The decade called for the church to be what some called a "moral community," actively opposing all forms of violence against humanity and against the environment. Being a "moral community" is not about standing apart from the world, offering tokens of support, but rather about being mixed up with the brokenness in the world, alongside and in suffering solidarity with it.[42]

There were high hopes when the Ecumenical Decade of the Churches in Solidarity was launched, that some of these questions would be addressed. Mercy Oduyoye writes, including a phrase from the letter to the churches from the then General Secretary of the WCC, Dr. Emilio Castro of Uruguay:

> The Decade is a challenge to the churches to demonstrate visibly and vividly that the forty years of WCC advocacy on behalf of women, and the many fine statements the Council has issued, are meant to change the actual life-styles and attitudes of churches and people toward women's "potential for promoting the vision of a new age in Jesus Christ," as Castro put it in his letter.[43]

The account of the work thus far celebrates the wealth of the programs that WCC has made available to women and to the churches; however, it begs the question, why issues of justice and inclusion that the Sexism Conference in Berlin in 1974 unearthed seemed to take a back seat by the time the Community

Study was completed and reported in Sheffield in 1981? Can this be possible that a section of the gathered women in Sheffield felt it important to draft a Statement reminding the conference that their struggles for survival and dignity are as important as the desire for a renewed church (the Third World Statement in the Sheffield Report).[44] Then again during the course of the Decade, the focus on "societal concerns" seemed to push ecclesiological challenges to the background. Is there really such a clean divide between those concerned with ecclesiological challenges and those concerned with the flourishing of life? Are not these two intermeshed concerns of women in the church and in society?

In Search of a New Ecclesiology

During the course of the Decade, women did call for a new understanding of what it means to be church as an ecclesiological question and not just as a question of justice for women.

> What women want is to build a new church, stripping it of its hierarchical and crippling institutionalism, so that it could indeed be a movement of concerned and involved men and women, engaged in a ministry of healing.[45]

What women were doing in their contexts, throughout the Decade, was to look for an alternative paradigm of the church. We are church, was the claim often made as women developed feminist spiritual and liturgical materials to respond to their struggles for dignity and for a violence free world. We are the church, women claimed as they developed more inclusive forms of worship and re-imagined and re-constructed symbols and doctrines of the church, to make them more meaningful to women's experiences. We are church, women claimed as they developed pastoral and theological resources to engage in movements for justice and for participation in political change. Mary Hunt describes the reaction of an octogenarian Roman Catholic woman when she heard Mary Hunt boldly assert that "We women are Church" on a radio program.

> Being church was a new concept for her, as it was for me, and for the thousands of other Roman Catholic women who affirm themselves as "church" despite the remarkable recalcitrance on the part of the kyriarchal institution to bring its structures and teachings in line with contemporary theological thought

and spiritual practice. Why and how we do so is an important chapter in church history. It is the story of power transformed.[46]

Being church! This was the spirit that I encountered as I traveled all over the world in the context of the Decade. Women of various denominations were saying just this. In other words, they were reclaiming their power to "transform" the church.

A new reflection and action process, "Women's Visions of the Church: Being Church," was only a next stage in the history of women in the ecumenical movement that attempted to delve into ecclesiological questions in the context of the growing women's movements in society and in the church. The core group which worked on this reflection process struggled hard to discover a title which embraces all the concerns it was to cover, so that it will make meaning to women and would bridge the seeming gulf between the church as an institution and the church as a community, facing the challenges posed by the world. The original title was "New Models of the Church." The majority of the Steering Group[47] that designed the process was happy with this title, but it was this, which provoked the most reactions, largely from colleagues from the Faith and Order stream of the WCC. Their argument was that such a title would be seen as interference in ecclesiological understandings of those churches for which the church is something inherited from tradition.

But then, the agenda of women in the ecumenical movement throughout the fifty years of the ecumenical movement was always about the integrity of the church to "be church" in the world. There has always been an attempt to avoid splitting the societal struggles of women (and did call on the churches to solidarity), from what could be described as more "churchy" issues. As Janet Crawford reminds us, right from the First Assembly of the WCC in 1948:

> Women insisted that the question of women's place in the church was a theological and ecclesiological issue, and it had to do with the very nature of the church and their membership in the body of Christ and, that woman's experiences in the churches were not to be ignored.[48]

The Community Study and the Decade, created the opportunity for the churches to listen to and learn from the insights of women as they explored in their different geographical and ecclesial contexts, fundamental questions about what sort of church God is calling us to be. What does it mean to be church in the world today? This was also one of the overarching concerns identified by the Central Committee for the whole of the WCC to address after the Assembly in Harare.

Mary Tanner analyzes the context in which the "Being Church" process was initiated:

> The insights of the Community Study and the Decade complement each other. The primary focus of the first was the internal life of the church; the primary focus of the second was on the church as it faces, and lives out, its calling in and for the world, particularly in attentive solidarity with women. The two belong together. As a result of the Community Study and the Decade of the Churches in Solidarity with Women, the ecumenical community in many places around the world has been helped to envision something of the church God calls us to be, and it has helped churches in some places to take steps, albeit small steps, to realize that vision. It is important to acknowledge this, for these are the stepping stones for the future, the foundation on which we can now build.[49]

The "stepping stones" to which Mary Tanner refers, i.e. the vision of the church that God calls us to be, contributed to the conclusions of the Women's Voices and Visions process that was brought to the WCC Assembly in Porto Alegre, Brazil, in 2006. The call to the churches was to take account of these voices and respond to women's deepest aspirations for community (*koinonia*), justice and solidarity. The hope was that out of this listening to, and engagement with women may come, renewal, transformation and greater unity of the churches.

As the final report of this process describes it:

> In discussing the meaning of "being church," women in regional groups frequently wanted to talk about "becoming church" as they talked of ways the churches could learn to stand in solidarity with the women who make up the majority of the membership of churches whose decision making is controlled by men. Gradually they began to realize that "being" is only one of at least three ways of discussing the reality of the church. One way of describing this is to talk about "the was-ness," "the is-ness," and the "shall be-ness" of the church. Answering the question, "What is the church for us today?" requires talking in

many tenses. The *Church [with a capital "C"] is what it was* as a gift of God in Jesus Christ, understood through the biblical and church traditions that witness to this gift of partnership and equality as seen in the relationships of the Trinity. The *church [with a small "c"] is what it is* as a plurality of structures and traditions that are seeking to become a people of God. At the same time *the church is what it shall become* as a sign of New Creation. The church is not just one of these tenses. We live in a present where we enter into ecumenical dialogue and pray, "God in your grace transform the church," yet give thanks for the gift of Christ's presence in the church, and long for a time when we will overcome the divisions and alienation within and between every nation and denomination.[50]

Recognizing that the focus of the discussion of women in all the regions was on the "is-ness of the church" and the experiences of women in those real and concrete church situations, we chose to drop the title, "being church" and instead to report on the voices and visions of how women envision the church they want. Women's understanding of the church comes directly out of their experience of Christian community in the midst of what are often the painful realities of their societies and in their daily lives. All the groups discussed the impact of globalization on their societies and on the lives of women and their families. They all stressed on the calling of the churches to be engaged in analyzing the social construction of gender that affects women in situations of war, poverty, ecological destruction, and the spread of HIV/AIDS. They were challenged to listen to and learn from young women's diverse perspectives on being church. The regional discussions spoke of how the churches do not live up to their calling to represent a full and just partnership of women and men of all ages.

THE WORLD COUNCIL OF CHURCHES AND ITS COMMITMENT TO WOMEN

This has been a history of commitment of women to the WCC and of the commitment of the WCC to women. Women have been on the agenda of the ecumenical movement from the early years of the last century, even when the idea of the WCC was just a concept. As identified in this book, every single Assembly of the WCC, beginning with the first one in 1948 in Amsterdam, referred in one way or the other to the role and status of women in the churches and on their rights and contributions. A brief look into the WCC archives will indicate that there has been no dearth of statements and recommendations regarding the place and role of women in the churches, made by the churches over the past over sixty years. But, the problem is that there is a wide gap between statements of solidarity and the actions that are actually taken. As Mercy Amba Oduyoye described it:

> Within the membership of the WCC, solidarity with women is a tenuous factor. Recommendations painfully made on this issue seem to apply only to the churches-in-council and not to individual member churches. Solidarity with women means different things for different churches. That is why the Decade efforts take different forms. Sometimes one is inclined to wonder whether the churches are in solidarity with the Council on this issue. Agreements on principles do not match the practice of several member churches and often one is inclined to conclude that the Council and its members are not in one mind.[51]

But, in spite of this, major signposts along the way in the history of the WCC that have been described in this chapter mark what can be clearly perceived as commitment to women. All these are among the initiatives and activities of the WCC, within the purview of the work of a "Women's Program," that has survived the many structural changes WCC has undergone since it was formed in 1948. It reveals that there has been considerable investment of human and financial resources in raising the voices and visions of women and in creating for them the ecumenical space to demand their dignity and rights.

It is indeed a courageous re-imagining of the church and world that has emerged through the work with women of the WCC. On the one hand, there were the many creative ways in which women were responding globally to the violence and exclusion they experience in their churches and in society. A new spirituality was emerging, nurtured by the many new ways in which women explored, through rituals and symbols, their ways of being church in their own contexts. Additionally, there was the gift of theological voices of feminist and womanist theologians around the world who with authority and scholarship, and with deep passion brought to the table shifts in paradigms in ecclesiology. Of these, the work of Letty Russell and her image of the Church in the Round, or Elisabeth Schussler-Fiorenza's "ekklesia of equals" or Mary Hunt's "justice seeking friends" come immediately to mind.[52] And there are other models of "being church" that women have drawn inspiration and sustenance from—among them are the Women Church movement in parts of Asia, Europe and North and South America, and the Circle of Concerned African Women Theologians.

A watershed moment during the Decade was a global conference "Re-Imagining: a Global Theological Conference by Women" for women and men, an inter-faith conference of clergy, laypeople, and feminist theologians in 1993 in Minneapolis, USA. It grew out of mainly the Presbyterian Church of USA's response to the World Council of Churches' Ecumenical Decade. It brought together 2,200 people, one third of them clergy, and most of them women. Eighty-three men registered. Attendees represented sixteen denominations, twenty-seven countries, and most of USA. All presenters were women. The conference aimed to encourage churches to address injustices to women worldwide and promote equal partnership with men at all levels of religious life. In recognition of the view that traditional Christianity's male-centered language and images have often stifled and hurt women, organizers chose "re-imagining" as the theme. International theologians were invited to address the theme as it applied to God, Jesus, church, creation, community, and world. After four days of building community and freedom of discussion with like-minded women, hearing internationally recognized feminist theologians advance new ways of thinking about Christianity, and hearing God referred to with female pronouns, attendees reported having a transformational experience—which proved controversial in some quarters but liberating in others. The event certainly had a ripple affect among women in many parts of the world. "Reimagining" was part of that subversive history of women's struggles to be heard and for their spiritual and liturgical resources to be affirmed.

At the WCC's global conference on the Community of Women and Men in the Church held in Sheffield, England in 1981, Elisabeth Moltmann-Wendel's strong statement has stayed with us through the history of women in the ecumenical movement. She began her presentation, which she made along with her husband Jurgen Moltmann, with these words: "Church history begins when a few women set out to pay their last respects to their dead friend Jesus."[53] Whether the churches recognize this historical heritage that Elisabeth so clearly pronounced, is the question. When the Anglican Church in England or the Presbyterian Church in Korea discussed the question of the ordination of women to priesthood for over 100 years before it can be decided on, one wonders just how seriously the Church takes this history of Christian origins. In fact, as Carol Lakey Hess, the theologian, says, "Christian history has by and large been told from the vantage point of theological victors—men who have held religious power."[54] She continues,

> There are contained in our traditions subversive strands and hints, indicating that cracks in patriarchy have repeatedly opened. The views of most women, however, and those who have been denounced as heretics have either been left out as distorted or evidenced only in the reaction against them.[55]

Now, women have begun, in the last few decades, to expose this history and their significant participation in that history. It is a history that has gone unacknowledged, and regretfully has been systematically suppressed or simply trivialized and ignored, even in the ecumenical movement. In fact, as Janet Crawford points out, there seems to be two streams in the ecumenical movement because the ecclesiological challenges raised by women have been marginalized in the work of the Faith and Order. She writes,

> When will women's ecclesiological questions and challenges be reflected with full seriousness in the ecclesiological studies of Faith and Order? Or will there continue to be two "ecclesiological streams" within the ecumenical movement, a "women's stream" and a Faith and Order stream?[56]

When the WCC was constituted at the First Assembly in Amsterdam in 1948, in fact two streams of ecumenical engagement—the Life and Work movement and Faith and Order movement had been merged. (The third stream—the International Missionary Council joined the world body only in 1961 at the Third Assembly in New Delhi in 1961; and the fourth stream, the World Council of Christian Education joined in 1971.) In 1992, the then Justice, Peace and Integrity

of Creation Commission (of which the WCC's women's program was a part) called on the Faith and Order Commission to
engage with it in a study process on Ecclesiology and Ethics, on
the premise that, "The ecumenical movement suffers damage so
long as it is unable to bring the justice, peace and the integrity
of creation process (JPIC) and the unity discussion into fruit-
ful interaction." It also suggested that, "The unity movement
has, from its beginnings, wrestled with issues of ecumenical
social witness and action."[57] The series of documents on ecclesiology and ethics—Costly Unity, Ronde, Denmark, February
1993; Costly Commitment, Tantur, Israel, November 1994; and
Costly Obedience, Johannesburg, South Africa, 1996—came out
through meetings organized by the two commissions together.
The final of the series, Costly Obedience, summed up the vision of the whole process—"to break free of the dichotomy of
consciousness and effort these streams (ref. Faith and Order and
Justice Peace and the Integrity of Creation) have represented."

It asked that while the two streams go forward, it is important
that they see that their visions are interrelated. I quote a paragraph from the Statement on Costly Obedience.

> Such a goal cannot be reached by simply pasting together in
> the same paragraphs sentences in each of these two institutional
> languages, seeking to say the same thing first in one vocabulary
> and then in the other. The point is to break away from the ar-
> tificial division of perspective two distinctive vocabularies have
> represented. This calls for a vision, with language to go with it
> that substantially recasts the two perspectives into one.[58]

Surely, it is this same logic we need to use to answer Janet
Crawford's concern about the perceived parallel tracks of a
Women's stream and the Faith and Order stream in the WCC—
the ecumenical movement will never be complete if they
stay this way—the journey, hopefully, toward a united voice
continues.

Two Issues Explored Among Many

There are many issues that can be the entry point into reimagining a new future for women in the ecumenical movement and
in the churches and the world. This book will go deeper into
only two such issues that have engaged the work of the WCC

over its history—the first is the destructive power and persistence of violence against women in the world and in the church; and the second, the issue of ordination of women. Both these issues are not by any count straightforward and are fraught with contradictions and challenges, so the chapters of this book do not claim to have the last word—they are meant to open a discussion for continuing work. Second, the choice of these issues is not intended to indicate any attempt at prioritization—they were selected as they are examples of how the diversity of traditions, social locations and experiences of women make our coming together as women in the ecumenical movement such a challenge. We as women cannot be categorized as "we the women of the ecumenical movement"—such a universalization of women has been one of the obstacles on our way as women. I will address that in the following chapters.

ENDNOTES

[1] Easter Message for the launch of the Ecumenical Decade of the Churches in Solidarity with Women, quoted by Mercy Amba Oduyoye, *Who Will Roll the Stone Away? The Ecumenical Decade of the Churches in Solidarity with Women* (Geneva: WCC Publications, 1990), 14.

[2] Muna Kaldawi-Killingback, *Women in the World YWCA Mother of the Ecumenical Movement* (quoting Carol Seymour-Jones, Journey of Faith: The History of the World YWCA 1945-1994), in *With Love and With Passion. Women's Life and Work in the Worldwide Church*, eds. Elisabeth Raiser, Barbara Robra (Geneva: WCC Publications, 2001), 121.

[3] Quoted by Susannah Herzel, *A Voice for Women: The Women's Department of the World Council of Churches* (Geneva: World Council of Churches, 1981), 7.

[4] From *The Interim Report of the Study on the Place of Women in the Church*, 1948 (Geneva: World Council of Churches), 9.

[5] Pauline Webb, *She Flies Beyond, Memories and Hopes of Women in the Ecumenical Movement*, RISK Book Series (Geneva: WCC Publications, 1993), 14.

[6] Visser't Hooft, quoted by Herzel, A *Voice for Women,* 12.

[7] Mossie Allman Wyker, "Reflections on the Past Ten Years, Reflecting on the Calibre of the Women Engaged in the Department's Work." Quoted by Herzel, A *Voice for Women,* 38.

[8] Herzel, A *Voice for Women,* 64.

[9] Webb, *She Flies Beyond,* 20.

[10] Pauline Webb, then Vice-Chairman (*sic*) of the WCC Central Committee, was moderator of the global conference. In her Introduction, *Report on Sexism in the 1970s: Discrimination Against Women* (Geneva: WCC Publications, 1975), 10.

[11] Webb, at the opening session of the conference, "Sexism in the Seventies," 10.

[12] Working Group Reports, *Sexism in the Seventies,* 97.

[13] Working Group Reports, *Sexism in the Seventies,* 103.

[14] Working Group Reports, *Sexism in the Seventies,* 103.

[15] Working Group Reports, *Sexism in the Seventies,* 111-112.

[16] *Nairobi to Vancouver, 1975-1983, Report of the Central Committee to the Sixth Assembly of the WCC* (Geneva: WCC Publications, 1983), 204.

[17] *Nairobi to Vancouver, 1975-1983,* 204.

[18] Melanie May, "Community of Women and Men in the Church," *Dictionary of the Ecumenical Movement,* eds. Nicholas Lossky et al. 2nd Edition (Geneva: WCC Publications, 2002), 235.

[19] May, "Community of Women and Men," 235.

[20] May, "Community of Women and Men," 234.

[21] Faith and Order Paper No. 151, *Church and World: The Unity of the Church and the Renewal of Human Community,* Faith and Order Study Document (Geneva: WCC Publications, 1990).

[22] Faith and Order Paper No. 151, 52.

[23] Faith and Order Paper No. 151, 52.

[24] Constance Parvey, ed., "Acknowledgements and Thanks," *The Community of Women and Men, The Sheffield Report* (Geneva: WCC, 1983), ix.

[25] "Third World Statement—European Response, Women and Men in Community for Humanity," *The Sheffield Report 1983,* 96.

[26] "Third World Statement—European Response," 96.

[27] Ranjini Rebera, *We Cannot Dream Alone: A Story of Women in Development,* Introduction (Geneva: WCC Publications, 1990).

[28] Athena K. Peralta, *A Caring Economy. A Feminist Contribution to Alternatives to Globalization Addressing People and Earth (AGAPE)* (Geneva: World Council of Churches, Justice, Peace and Creation Team, 2005).

[29] Meeting of the WCC Central Committee, Minutes, Dresden, Germany, 16-26 August 1981, 14-25.

[30] Webb, *She Flies Beyond,* 26.

[31] Bertrice Wood concluding the Plenary on the Ecumenical Decade of the Churches in Solidarity with Women, VIII Assembly, Harare, Zimbabwe, 1998. http://www.wcc-coe.org/wcc/assembly/decpl-e.html. accessed April 13, 2019.

[32] Press Release at the Decade Festival in Harare, November 1998. www.wcc-coe.org/wcc/assembly/festiv-e.html accessed April 13, 2019.

[33] Musimbi Kanyoro, at the opening worship of the Decade Festival, "Your Story is My Story, Your Story is Our Story," *The Decade Festival, Harare,* November 1998. (Geneva: Justice Peace Creation Team, WCC, 1999).

[34] Kanyoro at the opening worship of the Decade Festival.

[35] Press Release at the Decade Festival in Harare, November 1998, www.wcc-coe.org/wcc/assembly/festiv-e.html accessed April 13, 2019.

[36] Press Release at the Decade Festival in Harare, November 1998, http://www.wcc-coe.org/wcc/assembly/04pre.html accessed April 13, 2019.

[37] Press Release at the Decade Festival in Harare, November 1998, http://www.wcc-coe.org/wcc/assembly/04pre.html accessed April 13, 2019.

[38] Aruna Gnanadason in an interview. www.wcc-coe.org/wcc/assembly/festiv-e.html. accessed 13 April 2019.

[39] Gail Allan, "Piecing Hope: The Ecumenical Decade of Churches in Solidarity with Women and Justice for Women in Canada" (DTh thesis, Emmanuel College/Victoria University and the University of Toronto, 2004). Unpublished thesis shared by the writer with the author in June, 2014.

[40] Allan quoting Eileen Scully, "Solidarity: Love that Moves Hands and Feet," Groundswell Summer/Fall 1996, 3-4.

[41] Allan quoting Omega Bula, Groundswell, Spring 1998, 23-24. "Solidarity: Love that Moves Hands and Feet."

[42] Mary Tanner, "On Being Church: Some Thoughts Inspired by the Ecumenical Community," *The Ecumenical Review* 53, no. 1 (January 2001): 67.

[43] Oduyoye, *Who Will Roll the Stone Away?*, 50.

[44] "Third World Statement—European Response," *The Sheffield Report,* 96.

[45] Aruna Gnanadason, "The Church in Solidarity with Women: Utopia or Symbol of Faithfulness?" in *Feminist Theology in Different Contexts*, eds. Schussler Fiorenza Elisabeth and M. Shawn Copeland, Concilium 1996/1, (Maryknoll, NY: Orbis and London: SCM, 1996).

[46] Mary E. Hunt, "We Women are Church: Roman Catholic Women Shaping Ministries and Theologies," in *The Non-Ordination of Women and the Politics of Power,* eds. Schussler Fiorenza Elisabeth and Herman Haring (London: SCM Press; Maryknoll: Orbis Books, 1999), 102.

[47] The Steering Group was comprised of Mercy Amba Oduyoye and Elizabeth Amoah, from Ghana; Letty Russell and Shannon Clarkson from USA; Sophie Deicha from France; Christina Breban from Romania; Isabelle Graessle from Switzerland; Chung Sook Ja from Korea and Janet Crawford from Aotearoa/New Zealand, with Aruna Gnanadason as staff.

[48] Janet Crawford, "Women and Ecclesiology: Two Ecumenical Streams?" *The Ecumenical Review* 53, no. 1 (January 2001): 14.

[49] Mary Tanner, "On Being Church: Some Thoughts Inspired by the Ecumenical Community," *The Ecumenical Review* 53, no. 1(January 2001): 68.

[50] This report of the brief process was drafted by the Steering group of women with Letty Russell as the chief drafter. Unpublished manuscript in the WCC files, Geneva.

[51] Oduyoye, *Who will Roll the Stone Away?*, 44-45.

[52] See Russell, *Church in the Round: Feminist Interpretation of the Church* (Louisville: Westminster/John Knox Press, 1993); Schussler-Fiorenza Elisabeth, *In Memory of Her: A Feminist Theological Reconstruction of Christian Origins* (Reprint, New York: Crossroad, 1983); Mary Hunt, *Fierce Tenderness: A Feminist Theology of Friendship* (New York: Crossroad, 1992).

[53] Elisabeth Moltmann-Wendel and Jurgen Moltmann, "Becoming Human in New Community" in the section of the report entitled, "1354 Years from that Easter Day," The *Community of Women and Men in the Church: The Sheffield Report*, ed. Constance F. Parvey (Geneva: WCC Publications, 1983), 29.

[54] Carol Lakey Hess, "Education as an Art of Getting Dirty with Dignity," in *The Arts of Ministry: Feminist-Womanist Approaches*, ed. Neuger Christie Cozad (Louisville, Kentucky: Westminster John Knox Press, 1996), 80.

[55] Hess, "Education as an Art," 80.

[56] Crawford, "Women and Ecclesiology: Two Ecumenical Streams?" 22.

[57] Statement on "Costly Unity" (Meeting in Ronde, Denmark, February 1993) in *Ecclesiology and Ethics: Ecumenical Ethical Engagement, Moral Formation and the Nature of the Church*, eds. Thomas F. Best and Martin Robra (Geneva: WCC Publications, 1997), 2.

[58] Statement on "Costly Obedience" (Meeting in Johannesburg, South Africa, June 1996), in *Ecclesiology and Ethics: Ecumenical Ethical Engagement, Moral Formation and the Nature of the Church*, eds. Thomas F. Best and Martin Robra (Geneva: WCC Publications, 1997), 72.

CHAPTER 3

THE ORDINATION OF WOMEN TO PRIESTHOOD: DILEMMA OR PROMISE

> We will continue our exploration into what being church means for the world today as we strive for new models of leadership—ready, responsive and courageous; caring, loving and compassionate; inclusive, hospitable and embracing. . . . so that the Church will be each day truly the Church of Jesus Christ. We as women, as the Spirit leads us, will pour our ointment on the feet of the church.
>
> Aruna Gnanadason[1]

Throughout the history of the World Council of Churches, the question of the participation of women in the life of the churches has been a central commitment. It is certainly not possible or good to generalize the situation of women in all churches, however, women in different places and contexts have said that their leadership and spiritual gifts are not honored adequately by their churches. As the composite report of the Living Letter's visits to the churches during the Ecumenical Decade of the Churches in Solidarity with Women describes it:

> Women are a majority in most congregations and participate strongly in the spiritual and liturgical life of the church. They are active in parish life through a wide variety of lay ministries—*diakonia*, fund raising, teaching and counseling. They gain strength and satisfaction from all these kinds of participation and even if their contribution is not always recognized and they are unable to attain leadership in these areas. *Diakonia* provides good opportunities for valuable participation, including access to the ecumenical movement.

On our travels we also met women—feminist theologians and lay women—who are ready to assume new roles in the church. These women are determined to draw out the liberating strands of their faith. Some have found no place in the church to nurture their spiritual questioning and after much frustration, have started alternative church movements, new ways of being the church, of expressing their spirituality. It could be said that, rather than these women leaving the church, it is the hierarchical church which has left them.[2]

Women have spoken of the glass ceiling that blocks their upward mobility in leadership and the slippery floors that restrict and stifle their uninhibited and creative participation. There is evidence in the work of the WCC that the question of the ordination of women to priesthood is not by any standard the most important issue that has gripped the attention of women in the churches and the ecumenical movement in the last sixty odd years. In fact, it is only occasionally discussed as women grapple with more fundamental questions regarding their life and witness in the church and their prophetic role in society. Feminist theologians have questioned any static understanding of the orders of the church. Letty Russell, for instance, writes,

> The orders of the church can also be dynamic and changing in their responsibility to build up the community for its ministry in the world. Church historians and theologians no longer hold that a particular pattern of ministry was established by Christ from the beginnings of the church. Rather, they search for ways to show that a particular church tradition represents a continuation of the basic Tradition of Jesus' life and ministry, and continuing presence through the Spirit in the life of the Church.[3]

Women from the Orthodox traditions would draw attention to the many ways in which women's ministries have been understood and affirmed in their churches—the exclusive focus on ordained ministry is questioned by some women theologians from Orthodox churches.[4]

The issue of ordination to priesthood, however, does deserve consideration because it has been an issue of importance to many women (including some women from Orthodox churches) and does come up both in discussions among women and as a point of tension, on occasion, in the work of the WCC. It has also been perceived as a threat to Christian unity—hence it is an important issue to consider in any review of the participation of women in the ecumenical movement. Discussions on the ordination of women have not been easy as many churches still have not recognized this call of women. Many women speak of their pain as they encourage their churches to recognize the spiritual and pastoral gifts they offer to the churches and their ministries. Feminist theologian, Melanie May, an ordained minister of the Church of the Brethren, who served on the Faith and Order Commission of the World Council of Churches draws attention to the link between women in ordained ministry and the unity of the church. She writes,

> Discussion of the ordination of women is threaded through the ecumenical movement in the twentieth century. This thread of discussion is, however, a slender one and has, at times, been all but unraveled by silence on the subject. Today, we seek to weave this thread more integrally into the search for the visible unity of the church, acknowledging that the visible unity of the church is predicated on the recognition of all baptized members and the recognition of all those who are called to ordained ministries. We cannot, therefore, achieve the visible unity of the church unless we are willing to talk together, in truth and in love, about the question of women's ministries, including the ordination of women.[5]

Earliest reference to the subject in WCC records is found in the report on the Life and Work of Women in the Churches that was prepared by a few women for the First Assembly of the WCC in Amsterdam, in 1948. The Report, referring to the ordination of women, states,

> Some churches, for theological reasons, are not prepared to consider the question of such ordination, some find no objection in principle but see administrative or social difficulties; some permit partial, but not full participation in all the work of the church. Even in the last group, social custom and public opinion still create obstacles. In some countries, a shortage of clergy raises urgent practical and spiritual problems. Those who desire the admission of women to the full ministry believe that until this is achieved, the church will not come to full health and power. We are agreed that this whole subject requires further careful and objective study.[6]

The fact that this was an issue recorded in the first ever official voice of women in the ecumenical movement is indicative that it has been for many women, an issue of vital importance. But then the reaction of Sarah Chakko, a Syrian Orthodox woman from India, who was asked to present the report, "who felt that the question of the ordination of women was only a minor part of the whole problem,"[7] captures well the complexity of this issue and the unfinished discussion in the ecumenical movement.

THE COMMUNITY STUDY AND ITS REFERENCE TO THE ORDINATION OF WOMEN

The Community of Women and Men Study that is referred to in the previous chapter, which had culminated in a major conference in Sheffield in 1981 had explored three major areas— theology, participation and relationships—all three areas where change was urgently needed. The process had reiterated that "The unity of the church requires that women be free to live out the gifts that God has given them and to respond to their calling to share fully in the life and witness of the church."[8] The process was an ecclesiological study and had focused on the recognition that "women's issues" are issues concerning the *wholeness* of the *whole* church; a study of church unity with particular reference to the experiences of women. As a result:

> Significant ecclesiological challenges emerging from the study included questions about the structures of the church, about how power and authority were exercised and by whom. The question of power and exclusive leadership inevitably brought up the controversial questions of the ordination of women to the priesthood and the episcopate. Although there was no agreement on the answers to these questions, at Sheffield, they were clearly, and often painfully, articulated.[9]

The discussion on the ordination of women in the Community Study recognizes,

> the complexity and diversity of the existing situations both within and between the different churches. The state of the discussion is also at different stages in different cultures. Amongst the churches, there is a plurality of practice embracing those who do ordain women, those who do not, and those who are hesitant for ecumenical reasons.[10]

The report goes on to say that as knowledge of theology and sociology develop,

> we are offered a chance to deepen our understanding and practice of ministry and our relations with one another . . . . The issues involved in this matter touch us at our deepest level, embedded as they are in liturgy, symbolism and spirituality. There can be no real progress if church, state or any group within the church seeks to force a change in practice without taking this into account.[11]

The Community Study also points to the fact that the problems of ministry are related "to the social and cultural context where the identity of the church and individual Christians is being constantly challenged."[12]

Women from all parts of the world have described their own struggles with their churches on this concern. They have challenged their churches for blaming the patriarchal cultural contexts of their societies as the basis for excluding women. Musimbi Kanyoro gathers together some of these voices from Asia, Africa and Latin America in the book entitled, *In Search of a Round Table*. She writes about African women, where alternatively,

> The powers of healing, preaching and spiritual direction, typically understood by the Christian church to be priestly duties, are powers traditionally exercised by women and men in African societies. If there is to be any general picture of African women in ordained ministries, an inclusive study of the religious roles played by women in different types of societies in Africa is imperative.[13]

In the same book, Datuk Thu En-Yu from Malaysia makes a claim that women's roles in societies follow the path of Buddhism, Taoism and Confucianism impede their participation in ordained ministry.[14] So the stumbling block, in too many contexts, is the prevailing patriarchal culture rooted in religions rather than a well thought out biblically founded argument for the ordination or not of women.

BAPTISM, EUCHARIST AND MINISTRY PROCESS—ANOTHER OPPORTUNITY?

The Faith and Order Commission of the WCC engaged in an important process of reflection among the churches globally on issues related to Baptism, Eucharist and Ministry. This process culminated in Lima, Peru in January 1982, where the Faith and Order Commission gave final form to the convergence text entitled, "Baptism, Eucharist and Ministry (BEM)." It marked points of "theological convergence among the churches on issues which traditionally caused division among the churches."[15] It was at this same meeting that the final report of the Community Study was also received. However, "regretfully, the BEM document does not treat the ordination of women to priesthood in the main part of the ministry text but considers the issue in a commentary that gives a short description of the positions of churches that ordain women and those which do not."[16] Janet Crawford however, feels that the BEM text was not entirely uninfluenced by the Community Study. She writes,

> In both the baptism and Eucharist sections of the text, there are "theological insights about unity, equality and the imaging of Christ in us all" which, at least implicitly, makes connections to the Community Study and which may signal to women that they are "partners in the search for the visible unity of the church." It is in the section on ministry that the lack of connection between BEM and the Community Study becomes most obvious. The whole controversial issue of the ordination of women is dealt with in two carefully formulated and balanced paragraphs which conclude that: "An increasing number of churches have decided that there is no biblical or theological reason against ordaining women, and many of them have subsequently proceeded to do so. Yet many churches hold that the tradition of the church in this regard must not be changed." (BEM, "Ministry" Para. 18)[17]

She continues,

> In the much-praised Lima text itself, little attention has been paid to what was described as "the most obvious point of present and potential disagreement, namely, the ordination of women." (Cardman, BEM and the Community of Women and Men Study, *Journal of Ecumenical Studies*, 21 Winter 1988). Rather, on this point it seemed that Faith and Order had retreated from its bolder statements. The result satisfied neither opponents nor proponents of women's ordination and did little to advance dialogue between the two. BEM gave no lead to the vital and church-dividing question of women's ordination.[18]

Women as Ordained Clergy Can Make a Difference[19]

A year after the first women were ordained by the Church of England in 1994, a magazine commented,

> (In 1994) 38 women were ordained in the Church of England. In 1995, the total is more than 1400, constituting one-tenth of clergy in that church. The Anglicans have observed an increase in religious practice in parishes where a woman priest officiates, the number of parishioners increased by between 10 to 30 percent following the calling of a woman to serve as parish priest.[20]

In other words, women as priests can make a difference. It is true that for some churches the problem is theological or is not part of their inherited Tradition—but many other churches are re-examining the heart of their faith and have found theological and spiritual resources and insights, which have led them to ordain women. At the same time, I would state clearly, right away, that in this process we as women need to contribute to the redefining, refining and reconstructing of what priesthood is all about. We need to constantly challenge those who would still hold on to an understanding of the clergy "as an authoritarian sacerdotal caste with only formal ties to a community."[21]

We live in a world of exclusion and violence; a world with untold forms of discrimination that threaten the integrity of communities; a world that constantly poses difficult moral and ethical choices to men and women; a world where secular forces are strong, and spirituality is undermined; a world where religious fundamentalism runs rife and religion is used to legitimize communal identities leading to conflicts. Additionally, in the life of the church itself, increasingly there is evidence of gender-based discrimination and even of sexual abuse of women in pastoral contexts and more recently of the new steps the church has been called to take in the face of increasing evidence of pedophilia. In such a context, what should "ordained ministry" be about? The church is called to respond with compassion and pastoral fortitude. At the heart of the commitment to the ordination of women and men must be the concern for the community in which the church is present to serve. Therefore, women in ordained ministry must be viewed within the framework of "partnership or community rather than in isolation, because of the desperate needs of the people and the earth. Everywhere one turns there is reconciliation to be made, bodily and emotional wounds to be healed, relationships to be righted, wrongs to be amended and simple acknowledgement to be made."[22] Ordained ministry of women can be a "way to subvert the church into being the church,"[23] as Letty Russell describes it. She says this in the context of her own experience as an ordained woman for thirty-five years as the minister of a poor community church in East Harlem.

Constance Parvey concludes a workbook on the Ordination of Women in Ecumenical Perspective with these words:

> Church and ministry have always been intertwined and so ecumenical discussion about the ordination of women and men must include issues of both authority and wholeness. While the church must have supervision inside its ministry, outside it must live in solidarity with those who are most in need . . . debate on the ordination of women should not be yet another stumbling block to unity. In the struggle against division and injustice at all levels and in all forms in church and society, this debate can be an occasion to analyze and clarify existing models of faith and witness and an opportunity, in common purpose, to evolve new ones.[24]

It was a new model of leadership that I was privileged to witness at the consecration of the third woman bishop of the Lutheran Church in Germany in 2001,[25] Bishop Bärbel Wartenberg Potter, who had designed most of the liturgy for her consecration ceremony. The most moving part of the afternoon was the time for the laying on of hands. Among those who laid their hands on her to bless her were the two other women bishops in Germany,[26] along with male bishops from German churches and bishops from Papua New Guinea, Latvia, India, and the UK, among others. But there was also Marie Dilger, a housewife and friend of Bishop Wartenberg Potter. All of them invoked the Holy Spirit to lead her on in her ministry. The new bishop was not only received into the Lutheran Church of Holstein-Lübeck, but she was received into the community of the church, a global community, a community that goes beyond ecclesial boundaries. She started her ministry with manifold blessings—the blessings of God, the blessings of the community and the blessings of women. The words and a garland of flowers offered by the women of the Diocese symbolized this. This ceremony came after her formal election and approval of her election by the women and men of that diocese. Her community or "her congregation" was in prayer with her, as she acknowledged her servant-hood to them.

CALL/VOCATION

Most women who are ordained and those who are in dialogue with their churches on the issue of the ordination of women would speak of how they have been called to this vocation. Some women are concerned that the church abuses the concept of the call as a way of "keeping women in their place"—ecclesial authorities tell women that they are called to diaconal or other ministries and not to priesthood. Nancy Duff writes that, "The doctrine of vocation affirms that every individual life with its unique combination of gifts and limitations has divinely appointed purpose and that we are called to glorify God in all we do."[27] She continues later in the same text, "Although the doctrine of vocation can be misused to counsel tolerance for oppressive situations, if rightly interpreted it challenges oppressive conditions."[28] With women, there is a difference in their understanding of the calling or a vocation. In India for instance, many women enter theological schools, as a first choice, fully aware that they have no guarantee of ordination, or even of a job, and even if their churches will ordain them, they have no assurance that local congregations will accept them as priests. They enter anyway, with the conviction that it is a call they cannot ignore.

In a collection of personal testimonies, on *Women in the Ministry*,[29] every woman contributor refers to her ordination as a response to her vocation. Some of these voices: Alison Fuller of the Scottish Episcopal Church speaks of the denial of her vocation by the Church as the denial of women's humanity before God; Elizabeth Wardlaw of the Church of Scotland compares her vocation, her calling to that of Paul on the road to Damascus; Margaret Forrester ordained by the United Reformed Church speaks of being aware "of an overpowering sense of vocation which every church in which I worshipped had refused to recognize. The frustration and pain of this was sometimes hard to bear." Jean Mayland of the Church of England writes: "I had come to believe that I had a vocation to the priesthood when

I was in my teens, but of course I was told this was completely impossible. I was brought up in a high Anglo Catholic church where my faith was nurtured, and my vocation spurned."[30]

TAKING THE RISK . . . RESPONDING TO A CALL

I dwell here on what Jean Mayland has written because I knew her for many years, working with her in governing bodies of the WCC. After her long struggle, she was finally, one of the first of the thirty-eight women ordained by the Church of England. She describes her journey toward ordination:

> During my theology year I went for a selection conference and was accepted to train as a "Lady Worker" in the Church of England. On reflection I felt I could not face all the limitations and frustrations that would be involved in that work. I felt called to priesthood and not to "lady worker ship." I do so admire those women who moved in and worked as "lady/ women workers," and later as deaconesses. With courage and patience, they pushed back the boundaries. I could not have done it. I would either have exploded or have been destroyed and embittered by frustration.[31]

Jean Mayland got into the fray and, with other women, accompanied her church on the way to the final decision to ordain women. She speaks of how she, "along with my sister priests, have had to campaign and also fight with our church long and hard. Yet I love the Church of England with every fiber of my being."[32] In 1992, she was one of the few privileged women (having won in the ballot for tickets), to be able to sit in the gallery of the Church House and witness the debate and final approval of ordination of women to priesthood. Jean Mayland remembers,

> I managed to overcome my urge to burst into tears and expressed my joy and delight that after all these years this had happened . . . .The words that came to my mind were those of Siegfried Sassoon's poem about Armistice Day, which concludes "and the singing will never be done."[33]

But, there was not much space for singing after that—things did not go with the smoothness women hoped for. The press, who wanted to sensationalize the news about the ordination, especially because there was enough awareness of the opposition to it, constantly misquoted her. Some of the bishops and senior staff seemed to be more concerned about keeping in the church those who opposed the ordination, than to celebrate with the women their success. Even deans and canons showed their hostility. Family obligations did not make life easier. Jean Mayland was not able to take up full time ministry. While the earlier quotation from a magazine indicates that the ordained women in the Anglican Church of England did bring change in some congregations, it is also true that a few years after the decision to ordain women, many did not get parish ministries, and they had to go into specialized areas of work of the church or accept assistant posts.

Jean Mayland continues, "I am eternally grateful to God, with whom I often wrestle, that along the mysterious path of life where the going is often so dark, She has brought me on occasions to sit in places of stimulation, or of tranquility and joy."[34] Jean speaks of the deep emotions she experienced the first time she celebrated the Eucharist, "When I began the Eucharistic Prayer I felt I would not be able to get through it without collapsing into tears . . . .Never will leading the people in making Eucharist lose its humbling thrill, but never again will it be such an awe-inspiring privilege as that first time."[35]

I have traced the struggles and joys of one woman in one of the member churches of the WCC who has gone through such a complex experience in responding to what she declares is her calling—it is these women we have at the center of our thoughts, when we speak of the ordination of women. One meets women like Jean Mayland in every part of the world—women who so love the church that they are willing to put their lives and those of their families on the line, for the sake of what they believe in intensely. Women who come after them, for whom ordination is now a given, will not be able to fathom what price their "fore-sisters and mothers" have paid.

The teams who visited the member churches of the WCC at the mid-point of the Ecumenical Decade of the Churches in Solidarity with Women, (1994-1996) met with women and men and ecumenical communities all over the world. Inevitably, ordination of women to priesthood did come up in several places. The report of the team visits, the Living Letters, records that:

There are churches in all regions which forbid the ordination of women, even where they can cite no doctrinal or theological reasons why this should be so. While some churches recognize women's gifts, many are quite slow and even resistant to recognize and support women in ministry. Even where women have—after much struggle—been trained and ordained, fair pay, stable placements and moral support as they exercise their ministry are not guaranteed to them. After graduation, many women ministers must wait a long time to receive a posting. They may be forced to choose between vocation and family.[36]

THE CHALLENGE TO THE ECUMENICAL MOVEMENT

The women I speak of here are all from the World Council of Churches' membership churches and from the constituency the WCC serves from the Protestant tradition. At the Decade Festival (Harare, Zimbabwe, November 1998) that brought to conclusion the Ecumenical Decade, a letter was addressed to the WCC Assembly. In what I consider was a regrettable mistake, the issue of the ordination of women is referred to as "an ethical and theological problem" for the churches.[37] The drafters of the text left it this way to respect women from churches where ordination of women is not yet an issue. The strong requests from ordained women present were not accommodated. They urged that the paragraphs be redrafted with one paragraph focusing solely on the ordination of women. They wanted the text to highlight both their joys and their difficulties in ordained ministries. They asked that the text could also include a sentence that affirms that for some churches it is not an issue at all. However, the process did not allow for their voices to be heard and this left many women such as Jean Mayland as well as some women from the Orthodox churches disillusioned and unsatisfied. This convinced the WCC that there was need for further discussion on the ordination of women and a request was made to the Faith and Order Commission to re-engage the member churches on this issue.

THE QUESTION OF ORDINATION OF WOMEN AND THE UNITY OF THE CHURCH

"Openness to each other holds the possibility that the Spirit may well speak to one church through the insights of another"

(Baptism, Eucharist and Ministry text).[38] And yet, it has to be acknowledged that the issue of the ordination of women to priesthood has been one of the most divisive of issues for the churches. Mary Tanner, former Moderator of the Faith and Order Commission of the WCC, describes the dilemma clearly when she writes that among the churches that grew out of the Reformation, the movement to ordain women to full ministry of word and sacrament, coincided with the movement toward the visible unity of the church. The one has influenced the other. This result is not surprising, for the visible unity of the church involves the recognition not only of all its baptized members as members of a single community of faith but also of those who are called to be ministers of one communion.[39]

Mary Tanner continues, by quoting Anglican Archbishop William Temple who had as early as 1916 expressed a view which, she says, has been shared by many other committed ecumenists, "I would like to see women ordained. . . . desirable as it would be in itself, the effect might be (probably would be) to put back the re-union of Christendom—and reunion is more important."[40]

While the question of the ordination of women is certainly not easy, given the diversity of positions among the various church traditions that are part of the ecumenical movement, whether this discussion can be held responsible for the slow and arduous process toward visible unity is a matter of debate. It has to be acknowledged that there are several instances where the issue did affect unity discussions: the Anglicans did not join in the United Church of Canada in 1956 because that church ordained women. In the Anglican-Methodist unity scheme in England in the 1960s, the Methodists delayed the ordination of women till it was obvious that the unity scheme had failed. Even in the covenanting process that followed, involving the United Reformed Church, the Methodists, the Moravian and the Anglican churches, the ordination of women was once again an issue. The Church of England included a separate motion referring to the recognition of women ministers of other churches— this was defeated in the House of Clergy. There is occasional hope; at the Consultation of United and Uniting Churches in 1987, the situation was summed up in this way:

For some churches the ordination of women adds to the hindrances to unity; but the united churches are clear that further union for them is being made a more open possibility by the willingness of those to share the ordination of women which they have found to be a creative element in their common life.[41]

According to Mary Tanner:

The contribution of the WCC has been to help the churches to set the discussion within the context of an emerging convergence on the understanding of ministry and priesthood and, perhaps even more important, within the concept of the unity we seek. The studies on the unity of the church and the renewal of human community have enlarged and enriched the perspective of this unity. Some have come to maintain that the churches' ministry must include women in order to show to the world the depths of unity in human community and make the gospel and the vision of the kingdom credible in a broken and divided world. The unity of the church ought not to be set over against the unity of the human community.[42]

Melanie May had posed a similar question when she asked,

At the end, each and every one of us will need to search our hearts before God to discern whether we believe with Archbishop William Temple that visible church unity is "more important" than the ordination of women or whether visible church unity is at all achievable unless all baptized members— men and women alike in God's image—can fulfill the ministry to which God has called them in Christ.[43]

Even preceding the formation of the World Council of Churches, at the very first World Conference on Faith and Order in 1927 in Lausanne, the 400 church delegates, of which only 7 were women, had issued a prophetic motion which was accepted by that body. It is recorded in the Minutes: "The right place of women in the Church is one of grave moment and should be in the hearts and minds of all."[44]

The Third Assembly of the WCC in New Delhi, in 1961, called on the Working Committee on Faith and Order to set in motion a study on the theological, biblical and ecclesiological issues involved in the ordination of women. It was also stressed that the study be undertaken in close conjunction with the Department on Cooperation of Men and Women in Church, Family and Society.[45] The Working Committee of the Faith and

Order approved the proposal and decided to place the question of ordination of women on the agenda of the Fourth World Conference on Faith and Order to be held in Montreal, Canada, in July 1963.

> This decision was felt as necessary because the problem is of practical concern to an increasing number of churches. Many churches welcome women to the ordained ministry and have found the policy advantageous. Others, having adopted this policy, face serious tensions. In others, the policy is under discussion and provokes heated debate. The matter frequently becomes acute in negotiations for church unity. And even apart from formal negotiations, it affects the mutual relations of churches that ordain women to those that do not. It would be wrong, therefore, to view this issue as a result of feminist demands or agitation by a few enthusiasts. It concerns the total understanding of the ministry of the church and therefore has deep theological significance.[46]

This position spoken of over fifty years ago remains true till today, though in this period many churches have decided to and have ordained women to priesthood. It continues to be regrettable that some churches even today, view this deep longing of women to respond to their vocation as a campaign of a few feminists making unreasonable demands!

THE WORLD COUNCIL OF CHURCHES OFFERS AN ECUMENICAL SPACE

Konrad Raiser, then General Secretary in his report to the Eighth Assembly of the WCC in Harare, 1998, which also marked the end of the Ecumenical Decade of the Churches in Solidarity with Women spoke of the role of the WCC in providing a safe, ecumenical space for discussions such as those related to women. He said,

> In the uncertainty of the present situation, with its temptation to see identity in a defensive and exclusive way, the ecumenical movement needs to recapture the sense of the pilgrim people of God, of churches on the way together, ready to transcend the boundaries of their history and tradition, listening together to the voice of the Shepherd, recognizing and resonating with each other as those energized by the same Spirit. The World Council of Churches, as a fellowship of churches, marks the space where such risky encounter can take place, where

confidence and trust can be built, and community can grow. At present, this conviction is being tested severely by conflicts over moral issues, especially regarding human sexuality, and by the ecclesiological and theological challenges arising from the Ecumenical Decade of the Churches in Solidarity with Women. More than ever before, we need the WCC as an ecumenical space which is open and yet embraced by the faithfulness of God and protected by the bond of peace, a space of mutual acceptance and understanding as well as of mutual challenge and correction.[47]

In the discussion on the ordination of women within this ecumenical space, the most important criteria will be to discern the diversity of voices and opinions on the issue and to enter the discussion with sensitivity and respect for different ecclesiological backgrounds. It requires all parties to listen attentively to each other—to listen to the struggles over vocation. It is critical that in unity talks where "churches which take a more traditional view are contemplating union with churches which believe that in ordaining women they are led by the Spirit," the participating churches "seriously face the theological issues involved," and in this, "it is much to be hoped that whatever decision an individual church reaches there will be no accusation of heresy but that its decision will be accepted by others as a genuine effort to follow the guidance of the Holy Spirit."[48]

Additionally, we cannot undertake our discussion of the ordination of women or the ordination of men for that matter, without serious and sustained discussion of the ministry of all baptized members and the fact that some—women and men— are "set apart" or called to ordained priesthood. There has also to be further reflection on Christian anthropology and what it means when we affirm that male and female are created in the image of God. Perhaps most importantly of all, it requires an openness to the working of the Holy Spirit, in a reaffirmation of the doctrines, with the possibility of the development of the doctrines of the church in keeping with the times.

To women, the question of ordination is not simply of taking on a role which has been essentially a "male role," it carries within its discourse a commitment to reconstruct the vocation of priesthood. As Letty Russell describes it:

Feminists who experience the frustrations and problems of ministry and priesthood in its present form consider it to be part of the *male esse* of the church. They understand that the practice of ordained ministry in its present form is frequently bad for the well-being of the church and are calling for reexamination of ordination and of the ordering of church life.[49]

WITHER WOMEN OF THE ORTHODOX CHURCHES?

And as we discuss this issue, we are surrounded by a cloud of witnesses, women saints, ancient and new, who have been recognized by the church for the spiritual gifts they offer to the church—a "priesthood" of love, care and compassion that they have through the centuries offered to the church and human communities they served. They stand as our spiritual guides as we discuss this question. While the tradition of sainthood has been on the edges of the Protestant traditions and has accompanied us in our liturgical life, it is the Orthodox tradition that has offered this gift to the ecumenical movement. To Orthodox churches, women saints are not something out of the ordinary—because often, ordinary women who worked uncompromisingly and sacrificially for Christ and their communities have been elevated to sainthood. Ion Bria, a Romanian Orthodox theologian, describes the ministry of the saints to the church in this way:

> The faithful are called saints because of their participation in the holiness of God, who is holy by nature (Isa 6:3), in Christ (Phlm 4:21). They are "God's chosen ones, holy (or saints)" (Col 3:12). One aspect of the mystery of the church is this new consecration in Christ of a "kingdom of priests," "consecrated nation," "royal priesthood" (Exod 19: 6; Isa 43: 20-21; I Pet 2:9) which is not exclusive or restricted.[50]

This, among other things, is the tradition that has inspired women in the Orthodox Church to begin discussions on the ordination of women to the priesthood in their churches. I dwell here on the role Orthodox women have played in the ecumenical movement of women as their role is not often acknowledged—many a time they have felt marginalized, even ignored.[51]

The participation of Sarah Chakko of the Orthodox Church in India at the First Assembly of the WCC in Amsterdam (1948) and the pivotal role she played in the early formation of the WCC's Women's Program is a matter of pride. When researching her life and the role she played, I was fascinated that she held her own in the midst of powerful women and men leaders of the ecumenical movement in those early years—not only as an Orthodox woman, but as an Indian woman at a time in India where there were very few prominent women in the Indian churches.

There have been, throughout the history of women in the WCC, women of great courage and strength from Orthodox churches, of both the Eastern and Oriental traditions who have contributed significantly to the work. Elisabeth Behr-Siegel of the Ecumenical Patriarchate; Dimitra Koukoura representing the Ecumenical Patriarchate; Marie Assaad of the Coptic Orthodox Church; Mother Maria Rule, Russian Orthodox Church; Teny Pirri-Simonian of the Armenian Apostolic Church; Sophie Deicha, Leonie Liveiris, and Kyriaki Karidoyannes-Fitzgerald, all of the Ecumenical Patriarchate, Maha Milki Wehbe of the Patriarchate of Antioch; Tamara Grdzelidze of the Russian Orthodox Church, Christina Breban from the Orthodox Church in Georgia; Ancha-Lucia Manolache from the Romanian Orthodox Church, and Eleni Kasselouri-Hatzivassiliadi, Aikaterina Pekridou and Katerina Karkala Zorba from the Church of Greece are just some of the many women from Orthodox churches who have contributed to the work of the WCC.

I have been privileged to work with many of these women in the context of two major gatherings of women from the Orthodox churches organized in the context of the Decade in Damascus in 1996 and in Istanbul in 1997, in the Study process on Women's Voices and Visions of the Church and in many other programs of the WCC.

> I learned from my Orthodox sisters what it means for us as women to love the church and to respect its great traditions and yet speak with courage and conviction when something there disturbs us. All the women I met at these meetings are indeed gifts to the ecumenical movement. The Orthodox women spoke with sensitivity and respect and yet with boldness. It taught me that women can speak from within the tradition, yet

also speak to the tradition. And be part of the transformation of the tradition.[52]

It must be kept in mind that in Berlin at the Sexism in the '70s conference in 1974, 5 of the 150 women on the participants list were from Orthodox churches. At Sheffield, at the World Conference on the Community of Women and Men, out of the nearly 200 participants, 9 were from the Orthodox churches. Leonie Liveris, for instance, puts this to the "lack of response" from the church hierarchy in her book.[53] While this may be so, there is a question one can ask as to how the work of the women's program could have "missed" a section of its body and continued to claim to speak for the women of the ecumenical movement.

It is refreshing that the two conferences in the context of the Decade affirmed another reality. Kyriaki Karidoyanes Fitzgerald, the editor of the report of the two conferences, in presenting the final documents of the conferences, writes that they

> reflect the fact that the delegates regarded themselves as full members of the church. There is even as apparent ease and comfort about their identity as Orthodox women. But this way of taking their membership for granted also created a deep sense of responsibility among the participants "to speak the truth in love" (Eph 4:15) in the formal and informal discussions. This sense of accountability compelled them to call to attention certain practices in the church which compromise the gospel and impede the mission and witness of the church. The ramifications of sexism as sin were discussed in both conferences.[54]

The issue of ordination was addressed in the series of meetings of Orthodox women—all under the patronage of the leadership of the Orthodox churches—starting with the first in Agapia, Romania in 1976; Rhodes in 1988; Damascus 1996 and Istanbul, 1997. Some of the participants in the meeting in Damascus welcomed "the idea of organizing an inter-Orthodox conference on the ordination of women to the priesthood."[55]

Three important books have been offered by Orthodox women theologians to the discussions on women's participation in the life of the churches: Elisabeth Behr-Sigel's *The Ministry of Women in the Church*, published first in French in 1987 (Oakwood Publications, California); Kyriaki Karidoyanes

Fitzgerald's *Women Deacons in the Orthodox Church, Called to Holiness and Ministry*, published in 1998 and revised and re-published in 1999 (Holy Cross Orthodox Press, Massachusetts); and Elisabeth Behr-Sigel and Kallistos Ware's *The Ordination of Women in the Orthodox Church*, published in 2000 (World Council of Churches, Geneva). There is also *Many Women were Also There: The Participation of Orthodox Women in the Ecumenical Movement,* edited by Eleni Kasselouri-Hatzivassiliadi, Fulata Mbana Moyo and Aikaterini Pekridou, published in 2010 (World Council of Churches, Geneva and Volos Academy of Theological Studies, Volos, Greece).

Elisabeth Behr-Sigel refers to the new challenges within the Orthodox churches and describes one of the signs of the times as "a call that that we should discern between the living tradition and a fossilized traditionalism, particularly regarding the place of women."[56] She writes,

> As responsible theologians in the Orthodox Church—both men and women—have become aware of these contradictions, the question of the admission of women to a sacramental ministry has arisen. The question no longer comes to them only from outside in the course of ecumenical dialogue, but it has also become for them an internal problem.[57]

Many women of the Orthodox churches have been uneasy with the "dominating Protestant" voice in the discussion on ordination of women. By and large, it is a difficult discussion and one has to appreciate the commitment of some Orthodox women to keep it alive. Dimitra Koukoura, who teaches theology at the Aristotle University, Thessaloniki, draws attention to what is now called the Rhodes Consultation.[58] She writes,

> In relation to the issue of women's priesthood, the representative Rhodes Consultation proved beyond any doubt that this is not an inherent, burning and pressing demand of Orthodox women themselves. It is a speculation imported from outside, one that did not touch at the heart of Orthodox women; *but it is a matter, however, to which our church has an obligation to respond, because others have knocked on its door to hear its opinion.*[59]

It is an issue that has to be continued to be discussed among women in the ecumenical movement, respectfully and with a deep commitment to each other.

A Postscript: Ecumenical Deals and the Betrayal of Women?

I end this chapter with an account of a personal experience, to underline the struggles of women in the ecumenical movement when it comes to the question of the ordination of women. It was in 2001 when it was decided that I would have to withdraw from a commitment I had made several months earlier to speak at an International Conference on the Ordination of Women. This conference, organized by the movement called Women's Ordination Worldwide (WOW), focused on the Ordination of Women in the Catholic Church, and was held in Dublin. WOW was born out of the Ecumenical Women's Synod that took place in Gmunden, Austria, in 1996. WOW was described in the brochure announcing the conference as: "an association bringing together some of the groups working in different countries for the inclusion of women into a renewed priestly ministry in the Catholic Church."

Other speakers at the conference included the well-known Sr. Joan Chittister of the Benedictine Order and John Wijngaards, former priest, who have worked extensively on the question of the ordination of women to priesthood. While I had to withdraw from the conference, the other two speakers did participate. Sr. Joan Chittister participated amid threats from the Vatican, of expulsion from her Order. Her superiors supported her, and she announced that she was participating because "disobedience" was at the heart of the Benedictine Order of Sisters.

After many days of intense discussions around my participation and after a flood of email exchanges, I sent in a letter withdrawing my participation. As a staff person of the WCC, I could not act independently on occasions such as this—the decision to withdraw was not mine alone. When she heard of all that had transpired, Letty Russell who was my mentor in my doctorate of ministries program encouraged me to write a paper on what this implies for women in the ecumenical movement. I shared this paper with the then General Secretary of the WCC, Dr. Konrad Raiser, who wrote a personal handwritten note which describes, in my understanding, the complexity of the WCC's response. It is also a fine example of how seriously he took our work and women's struggles in the church. He writes,

87

I think that you succeed admirably to work through the pain and anger surrounding the decision to cancel your participation in the Dublin Conference. I am sorry that I was part of the "deal" and accept the critical challenges. But you go beyond this level of argument to the central theological and ecclesiological issues arising with regard to the alienation of women...I like very much the outline of the study process on new ways of being church.[60]

Why did the WCC have to take this position?

The WCC does not normally get involved in internal discussions of member churches, especially in matters related to faith and order, unless invited into the discussion. The WCC sees its role as being the initiator of discussions, and of providing the ecumenical challenge and the ecumenical space to bring together various theological and ecclesiological positions among member churches, so as to foster sharing and mutual accountability. What made my participation in the WOW Conference even more complex was the fact that the Roman Catholic Church is not a member church of the WCC. While it was possible for the other speakers to defy the Vatican and participate, for the WCC the question is not quite so simple. My participation was perceived as problematic, because it could be WCC taking "one side of the argument in a specific Roman Catholic debate" and could be understood as interference in a "very contentious inner-catholic discussion." As there is nothing in writing from the Vatican, we can only conjecture what the Vatican's "perception" of events was and the kind of pressures they were in themselves.

WCC/Roman Catholic relationships

My withdrawal must also be seen in the context of the history of the rather tenuous relationship between the WCC and the Vatican. The Fourth Assembly of the WCC (Uppsala, 1968) that came after the Second Vatican Council, raised strong hopes that the Roman Catholic Church (RCC) would become a member in the WCC. In 1969, Pope Paul VI said that the question of membership "contains serious theological and pastoral implications. It thus requires profound study and commits us to a way that . . . . could be long and difficult." The decision was taken not to apply for membership "in the near future," even if it was asserted that there were no insuperable theological, ecclesiological or canonical objections to membership.[61]

In 1965, a Joint Working Group (JWG) was set up to foster relations between the WCC and the RCC, which since 1980 has structured its agenda around the unity of the church; common witness; societal questions; and ongoing collaboration.

> The JWG endeavors to interpret: major streams of ecumenical thought and action as well as present successes and obstacles in common witness, relation between bilateral and multilateral dialogues, mission and evangelism, challenges of youth, Christian women in church and society, education (general and religious), mixed marriages, national and local councils of churches, ethical issues as new sources of division, human rights and civil liberty.[62]

The concern for "Christian women in church and society" is on this agenda but the fact remains that it has remained a point of contention. Relations between WCC and the RCC are not easy regarding several concerns and a great deal of sensitivity is required to maintain relationships. There must be a pragmatic recognition of the complex ecclesiological structure of the RCC, and of the possibilities of controversy between the universal and local churches. Ever since then, this has remained a point affecting WCC/RCC relations. Despite the RCC's official participation in the Faith and Order Commission and in the Commission on Mission and Evangelism and in their observer status in many other areas of the work of the WCC and in some regional and national councils of churches, issues such as the ordination of women to priesthood are not easily addressed.

Roman Catholic women, on the other hand, had another view on the events of June 2002. In an article in the *National Catholic Reporter*, Rosemary Radford Ruether explores various "ecumenical deals" that result in "the betrayal of women." She makes a comment on the events surrounding the 2001 WOW Conference:

> (This kind of) ecumenical deal was in evidence last summer when the Vatican was determined to block the international women's ordination conference in Dublin. Aruna Gnanadason was asked to withdraw, although she sent her speech to be read at the meeting. Thus, the Christian world was treated to the strange sight of Catholic women successfully resisting Vatican

orders while Protestants capitulated to them. Again, male church leaders assumed they should defer to the churchmen who reject women's ordination, rather than "offending" them. Offending and betraying women of one's own church apparently is not a matter of concern.[63]

While I could challenge some of the phrases Rosemary Radford-Ruether has used in this article, I agree with most of what she has written. The year 2001 did mark the 25th anniversary of the ordination of women in my own church—the Church of South India. Therefore, as I wrote in one of my email messages, as the decision for my withdrawal was taken:

> It has not been easy, and I have spent several sleepless nights wrestling with the issue. I do feel that this is the first time I have let down the women, including ordained women in my church who celebrate the 25th anniversary of the ordination of women this year.[64]

The Ecumenical Challenge

As the first part of this chapter underlines, the question of the ordination of women has been contentious within the family of the WCC member churches themselves. The WCC does not represent one ecclesiological tradition and the issue of the ordination of women has been viewed as an "obstacle" in ecumenical relations between member churches within the WCC and outside; and it has been a difficult and long struggle within individual churches. Most churches that now do ordain women had reached the decision only after years of discussion and negotiations led by women. Pauline Webb, a mother of the ecumenical movement and Methodist from the UK, wrote this to me when the decision of my withdrawal became public.

> When I heard you had withdrawn, I guessed there must have been a lot of pain and conflict involved in that decision. Yesterday, we had a Women's Forum during a lunchtime meeting at the Methodist Conference. The title was, "When I am old I shall wear purple" and the theme was the question of women bishops. I get so angry about the way ecumenism is used as an argument to prevent women from fulfilling their vocation. I remember way back when I started campaigning for the ordination of women in our church; someone quoted to me the words, "You women are another wound in the Body

of Christ." But as someone else responded, "It is by His wounds that the Church will be healed."[65]

It was a small group of women deeply committed to their church who decided to call for the Ordination Conference in June 2001 in Dublin. With almost no funds, and with a simple and poorly equipped office, these women came together and organized the gathering in Dublin. I met Myra Poole, the main designer of the event earlier and was amazed at her resilience and conviction that the event will take place, even when nothing was set in place. The women came not only with the authority of their experience but also with the authority of their vulnerability and unstinting faith. The commitment and courage of the women was, however, misunderstood and not honored by the church. There was every effort made to sabotage their efforts. It raises fundamental questions about the source of authority and power in the church. Letty Russell describes the dilemma we live with:

> As Christian women and men we are all very much caught up in this paradox. We continue to live in the old house of authority, the master's house, while at the same time seeking to understand just how Jesus cleansed that religious house so that it could become "a house of prayer for all the nations." (Mark 11:17)[66]

It is this that the organizers of the event did, as they continued till the end to "defy" patriarchal authority, and did hold the event they had planned in the first place. One wonders why the church was so afraid to allow the women to meet and have their discussion on the ordination of women. There was real anxiety because the website of the conference described the plan to make a petition to the Pope. Is the church afraid of the "cleansing of this religious house"? WCC's visible withdrawal only got them publicity that could have evaded the event, as it was to be a "small" meeting, tucked away in a corner of the world. Registrations poured in, as women found ways to resource themselves and to participate. The organizers managed to secure support to bring some women from other parts of the world to the event. Those who participated, told me that it was a wonderful event—one in a continuing discussion on ordination of women to priesthood, whether the church liked it or not, whether the church would continue to use its authority to stop such discussions or not!

To Letty Russell, "the call to ministry is not an option for some Christians. It is basic to the existence of all Christians as they seek to live together as partners in Christ's service."[67] Priesthood of all believers refers to the way we are church in the world today. It seeks to affirm a Christian community that lives in justice and in a world without violence. Justice and community are central to women in the way they model church. The challenge before us as women is to move the churches and the ecumenical movement "from solidarity to accountability."[68]

In Conclusion

It is appropriate to conclude this chapter with the words of Bishop Kallistos Ware, Bishop of Diokleia, who addresses the Orthodox churches, with words that are appropriate for all churches—those that ordain women and those, which do not. He writes,

> In discussing the ministry of women in the church, let us not be afraid as Orthodox to acknowledge that there is a mystery here which we have scarcely started to explore. In speaking of a "mystery," I am using the word in its proper theological sense. A mystery is not just an enigma or an unsolved puzzle. It is a truth, or a set of truths *revealed* by God to our created intelligence, yet never *exhaustively* revealed because it reaches into the depths of divine infinity. The primal mystery is always the incarnation of Christ (see Eph 1:9; Col 1:26-27), in which all other mysteries—including the *mysteria* or sacraments of the church, such as baptism, Eucharist and priesthood—find their origin and their fulfillment.[69]

Women will keep this discussion alive as they recognize that they need to continue in the search and discovery of the best way to offer their theological and spiritual gifts to the church and to the world.

ENDNOTES

[1] Aruna Gnanadason, "We Will Pour our Ointment on the Feet of the Church: The Ecumenical Movement and the Ordination of Women," written for a conference on Ordination of Women in the Roman Catholic Church, 2001. For this chapter, I have used extracts from the paper I was to read at the Women's Ordination Worldwide Conference, Dublin in 2000. http://www.womenpriests.org/related/gnanadas.asp.

[2] *Living Letters: A Report of Visits to the Churches during the Ecumenical Decade—Churches in Solidarity with Women* (Geneva: World Council of Churches, October 1997), 17-18.

[3] Letty Russell, *Church in the Round: Feminist Interpretation of the Church* (Louisville: Westminster/John Knox Press, 1993), 49.

[4] See for instance, *Orthodox Women Speak: Discerning the Signs of the Times*, ed. Kyriaki Karidoyanes Fitzgerald (Geneva: WCC Publications, 1999); and *Women's Voices and Visions of the Church: Reflections by Orthodox Women*, eds. Christina Breaban, Sophie Deicha and Eleni Kasselouri-Hatzivassiliadi (Geneva: WCC Publications, 2006).

[5] Melanie M. May, "A Survey of Faith and Order Discussions on the Ordination of Women: A Retrospective Introduction to Future Work," June 1, 1998, accessed April 15, 2019, https://www.oikoumene.org/en/resources/documents/wcc-programmes/ ecumenical-movement-in-the-21st-century/member-churches/special-commission-on-participation-of-orthodox-churches/sub-committee-ii-style-ethos-of-our-life-together/faith-and-order-on-womens-ordination.

[6] *Interim Report on the Life and Work of Women in the Churches* that was prepared by a committee of women for the First Assembly of the WCC in Amsterdam in 1948 (Geneva: WCC Publications 1948).

[7] Ans J. Van der Bent, *Vital Ecumenical Concerns, Sixteen Documentary Surveys* (Geneva: WCC Publications 1986), 192.

[8] David M. Paton, ed., *Breaking Barriers, Nairobi 1975: The Official Report of the Fifth Assembly of the World Council of Churches,* Nairobi, November 23-December 10, 1975 (London: ISPCK, London, 1976), 13.

[9] Janet Crawford, "Women and Ecclesiology: Two Ecumenical Streams?" *The Ecumenical Review* 53, no. 1(January 2001): 16.

[10] Constance Parvey, ed., *The Community of Women and Men, The Sheffield Report* (Geneva: World Council of Churches, 1983), 129.

[11] Parvey, *The Sheffield Report*, 129-130.

[12] Parvey, *The Sheffield Report,* 130.

[13] Kanyoro, "The Ordination of Women in Africa," *In Search of a Round Table*, *Gender, Theology & Church Leadership, (Geneva: WCC Publications, 1997)*, 150.

[14] Datuk Thu En-Yu, "Cultural Elements of Women's Ordination," *In Search of a Round Table,* 139-140.

[15] Crawford, "Women and Ecclesiology: Two Ecumenical Streams?" 17.

[16] Mary Tanner, "Ordination of Women," *Dictionary of the Ecumenical Movement*, eds. Nicholas Lossky et al., 2nd ed. (Geneva: WCC Publications, 2002), 856.

[17] Crawford, "Women and Ecclesiology: Two Ecumenical Streams?" 17.

[18] Crawford, "Women and Ecclesiology: Two Ecumenical Streams?" 19.

[19] Women's Ordination Worldwide Conference, Dublin in 2000.

[20] Christine Grumm, Quoting from the magazine of the Lutheran Church in Alsace-Loraine, France, *In Search of a Round Table,* 39.

[21] Brand Eugene L., in "Vocation and Ministry," *In Search of a Round Table,* 15.

[22] Gail Lynn Unterberger, "Ministry," in *Dictionary of Feminist Theologies,* eds. Letty M Russell and Shannon J. Clarkson (Louisville, Kentucky: Westminster John Knox Press, 1996), 184.

[23] Letty Russell, *Household of Freedom, Authority in Feminist Theology* (Louisville, Kentucky: Westminster Press 1987), 88.

[24] Constance Parvey, ed., *Ordination of Women in Ecumenical Perspective,* Postscript, Faith and Order Paper 105 (Geneva: World Council of Churches, 1980), 65.

[25] It was the beginning of World War II in Germany, men had to go to the front lines and women had to take on "men's roles" including the work of priesthood in parishes. Congregations asked that these women be ordained, so in Germany the first ordinations of women took place in 1943. In 1945, when men came back from the war and were ready to take up their roles, there was a question as to what to do with the women priests. The local church authorities deliberated the question and recognized that in ordaining these women, they had been led by the Holy Spirit and the decision was not revoked. However, it was only in 1972 that the official decision to ordain women was taken by the National Church in Germany (EKD). The first woman bishop, Maria Jepsen, was consecrated in 1992.

[26] Bishop Maria Jepsen and Bishop Margot Käßmann.

[27] Nancy J. Duff, "Call/Vocation," *Dictionary of Feminist Theologies,* 34.

[28] Nancy J. Duff, "Call/Vocation," 35.

[29] Lesley Orr Macdonald, ed., *In Good Company, Women in the Ministry* (Glasgow: Wild Goose Publications, 1999).

[30] Jean Mayland and other ordained women—the testimonies of several women are included in this collection. *In Good Company*, 25-189.

[31] Macdonald, *In Good Company,* 37.

[32] Macdonald, *In Good Company,* 47.

[33] Macdonald, *In Good Company,* 40.

[34] Macdonald, *In Good Company,* 43.

[35] Macdonald, *In Good Company,* 45.

[36] *Living Letters: A Report of Visits to the Churches,* 34.

[37] Letter to the Assembly from the women and men at the Decade Festival, *Your Story is My Story, Your Story is Our Story.*

[38] *Baptism, Eucharist and Ministry,* Faith and Order Paper 111, Geneva, WCC, 1982.

[39] Tanner, "Ordination of Women," 753.

[40] Tanner, "Ordination of Women," 753.

[41] Tanner, "Ordination of Women," 753.

[42] Tanner, "Ordination of Women," 754.

[43] May, "A Survey of Faith and Order Discussions on the Ordination of Women: A Retrospective Introduction to Future Work," Faith and Order Paper No. 185, 71.

[44] *Faith and Order: Proceedings of the World Conference, Lausanne August 1927,* ed. H.N. Bates (New York: George H. Doran Co. 1927), 372.

[45] Melanie May, referring to the section on "What Unity Requires," *Breaking Barriers. Nairobi 1975: The Official Report of the 5th Assembly of the WCC, 1975,* ed. David M. Paton, in *Bonds of Unity: Women Theology and the World-Wide Church* (Atlanta, Georgia: American Academy of Religion, Scholar's Press 1989), 3-4.

[46] Report of a Consultation on *The Ordination of Women: An Ecumenical Problem,* organized by the Department of Faith and Order and the Department on Cooperation of Men and Women (Geneva: WCC, May 1963), 5.

[47] Konrad Raiser, "Report of the General Secretary to the VIII Assembly of the WCC, December 1998," *The Ecumenical Review, Echoes from the Harare Assembly* 51, no.1 (January 1999), 89.

[48] Report of the Consultation on "The Ordination of Women: An Ecumenical Problem," 1963, 10.

[49] Letty Russell, *Church in the Round: Feminist Interpretation of the Church* (Louisville, Kentucky: Westminster John Knox Press, 1993), 50.

[50] Bria Ion, "Saints," *Dictionary of the Ecumenical Movement,* 890.

[51] Kyriaki Karidoyanes-Fitzgerald, "Orthodox Women in Theological and Ecumenical Context: Assessing Concerns for Today and the Future (The More Things Seem to Change, the More They Stay the Same?)," in *Many Women were Also There . . .The Participation of Orthodox Women in the Ecumenical Movement,* eds. Eleni Kasselouri-Hatzivassiliadi, Fulata Mbano Moyo and Aikaterini Pekridou (Geneva: WCC Publications; Volos Greece: Volos Academy for Theological Studies, 2010), 37-55.

[52] Kyriaki Karidoyanes Fitzgerald, ed., *Orthodox Women Speak: Discerning the Signs of the Times* (Geneva: WCC Publications; Brookline Mass.: Holy Cross Orthodox Press, 1999), Introduction, x.

[53] Leonie Liveris, *Ancient Taboos and Gender Prejudice: Challenges for Orthodox Women and the Church* (Ashgate New Critical Thinking in Religion, Theology and Biblical Studies), 2005.

[54] Fitzgerald, ed., *Orthodox Women Speak: Discerning the Signs of the Times,* 6.

[55] "Report of the Istanbul Meeting of Orthodox Women, May 1997" in *Orthodox Women Speak Discerning the "Signs of the Times,* ed. Kyriaki Karidoyanes Fitzgerald, 1999. (Geneva: WCC Publications), 34.

[56]   Elisabeth Behr Sigel and Kallistos Ware, *The Ordination of Women in the Orthodox Church*, RISK Book Series (Geneva: WCC Publications, 2000), 1.

[57]   Sigel and Ware, *The Ordination of Women in the Orthodox Church*, 8.

[58]   The Rhodes Consultation was held in 1988, under the patronage of the Ecumenical Patriarchate, and brought together representatives of the two families of Orthodox Churches to discuss, The Place of the Woman, in the Orthodox Church and the Question of the Ordination of Women. The proceedings edited by Gennadios Limouris were published by Tertios Publications, Katerini, 1992.

[59]   Dimitra Koukoura, "What Does it Mean to Live in the World and for the World?" *The Ecumenical Review* 53, no. 1(January 2001), 41.

[60]   Konrad Raiser, in a personal hand-written note dated May 2, 2002.

[61]   Marlin Van Aldermen, "WCC, Membership of," *Dictionary of the Ecumenical Movement*, 1991, 1099.

[62]   Tom Stransky, "Joint Working Group," *Dictionary of the Ecumenical Movement,* 550.

[63]   Rosemary Radford Ruether, *National Catholic Reporter*, December 14, 2001.

[64]   Email sent to the staff leadership group on May 8, 2001.

[65]   Pauline Webb, email dated June 28, 2001.

[66]   Letty Russell, *Authority in Feminist Theology: Household of Freedom* (Philadelphia: Westminster Press, 1987), 60.

[67]   Letty Russell, *Church in the Round: Feminist Interpretation of the Church,* 50.

[68]   Musimbi Kanyoro, Opening Speech at the end of Decade Festival, Harare, Zimbabwe in *Your Story is My Story, Your Story is Our Story—Report of the Decade Festival* (Geneva: WCC Publications, 1999), 29-36.

[69]   Kallistos Ware, "Man, Woman and the Priesthood of Christ," in *The Ordination of Women in the Orthodox Church*, eds. Elisabeth Behr-Sigel, Kallistos Ware RISK Book Series (Geneva: WCC Publications), 51-52.

CHAPTER 4

THE CHURCH AS A SANCTUARY OF COURAGE

Grace has come to us in unexpected ways, in the midst of life.
We have known healing, courage, restored love—salvation.
From these experiences of grace, we have arrived at a new
theology. We see how to live in resistance to violence; we see
how to live in love and truth without denying bitter realities.
We have learned how to use power, how to create places of
hospitality for human flourishing, how to be present, how to
choose life.

Rita Nakashima Brock and Rebecca Ann Parker[1]

WOMEN ARE NOT SAFE IN PEACE TIMES OR IN TIMES OF WAR AND CONFLICT AND EVEN IN THE CHURCH!

The year was 1991, the context—the setting of the Seventh
Assembly of the WCC in Canberra. It was the last day of the
Assembly when a young woman confided to friends that she
had been raped by a male participant at the Assembly site. It
came as a shock to all who were privy to this information in
the leadership. The usual accusations crossed many of the conversations—"It was her fault, she should not have opened her
door when she heard the knock"; "she asked for it, she was too
friendly with everyone," "it was a cultural misunderstanding."
But on the other side, there was strong outrage and protest that
the victim was being blamed, "she opened the door because
the voice outside was that of a new friend she had made at the
Assembly"; "she was caught unawares, he barged into her room

97

when she opened the door as a friendly gesture," "he took advantage of her vulnerability," "he deserves to pay for this crime." The young woman was given all the comfort and support that could be given to her at that time and she accepted the offer of counseling; but decided against any legal action that the WCC and the local hosts said would be provided, as she was eager to return home. Since the event had taken place on the last night of the Assembly, it was not possible for the WCC to do more at that time—discretion was required all around to protect the young woman who was the victim of this crime. The man's church was contacted by the leadership and he did face censure and was excommunicated from the church, when he returned to his home country. The young woman's home church accompanied her healing process.

This incident did challenge the WCC to become more vigilant—policies and procedures were put in place for responding to incidents of sexual harassment/violence on the level of governing bodies and in the context of all meetings of the WCC. Staff rules were amended to protect staff. A pastoral and educational brochure addressing the issue of sexual harassment/violence entitled, "When Christian Solidarity is Broken," was published and widely distributed. Every Assembly since then has had a version of this in the handbook of that Assembly. A well-advertised and announced pastoral group accompanies every Assembly to act immediately when required. A cautionary note that sexual harassment and violence will not be tolerated is announced to the Assembly. It was time these precautions were put in place—as it was not the first instance of sexual violence that had taken place in the context of an ecumenical gathering and the procedures have come in handy on one or two occasions even after 1991. It is a tragic flaw that such incidents could happen at all in the sanctity of the church and in the ecumenical movement.

The Bosnian War (1992-1995) saw thousands of women raped by soldiers of all ethnic groups—"rape as a weapon of war" is as old as war itself and it reared its ugly head once again in the context of that war. There were calls for WCC's intervention from European women, especially women from Switzerland and Germany who took the lead. Two ecumenical teams were formed—one to go to Serbia and the other to Croatia. The devastation that the war had caused in the lives of women was heart-rending. Both teams came back with accounts of destruction; of the tired, sad faces of women telling us stories of violence and rape and with strong appeals for solidarity. A fund was put in place, managed by women in the region to support survival efforts of the women and healing processes. There was also an appeal that the WCC promote and support the Women in Black movement—an initiative of the women in Serbia to propagate the message of peace and to put an end to rape and violence. This initiative had been inspired by the movement in Israel/Palestine when Jewish, Muslim and Christian women came together and marched or stood in silent protest to end the hostilities and all the violence in that region. Margot Käßmann, who was on the WCC's women's team to Croatia, urged that we link this struggle with the ongoing protests of the Mothers of Plaza de Mayo in Argentina, (*Asociación Madres de Plaza de Mayo* in Spanish) an association of Argentinian mothers, whose children "disappeared" during the military dictatorship, between 1976 and 1983. The mothers began their protests in 1977 marching in silence every Thursday, at the Plaza de Mayo in Buenos Aires in front of the presidential palace in public defiance, demanding the return of their children. (The movement continues as the Grandmothers of Plaza de Mayo).

In solidarity with the women engaged in these two struggles from two corners of the world—the WCC launched the Thursdays in Black Movement in the year 1993. At a busy intersection in Bangalore in India; on a roadside in Washington DC; in a church yard in Edinburgh; on a busy public thoroughfare in Sydney and in Manila—and in other places all over the world, women wear black and protest, as they hold up, in silence, posters and banners demanding an end to violence and rape in times of war and in times of peace. This campaign was re-launched by the WCC a few years ago and continues to be a way in which women keep up their resistance to violence and express their yearning for justice and peace in their lives and in the world. A few men join the movement in some places.

On December 6, 1989, a gunman Marc Lepine, opened fire on female students at the *Ecole Polytechnique* in Montreal, Canada after ordering the male students of the engineering class to leave. He had been refused admission to a course to study engineering and he showed his rage by firing at twenty-seven women students; as if they had no right to be there in what is perceived to be normally "a male domain." Fourteen of the women were killed—he then turned the gun on himself. The whole country, in fact the world, paused in shock thinking of the depth of anti-women sentiments this brutal act exposed. Outrage and grief turned into action and every year since then, these lives that had been lost so needlessly are honored through silent marches and vigils, discussion groups and worship events across Canada and in many other parts of the world. More than two decades later, their lives are still mourned. December 6 has been marked as the National Day of Remembrance and Action on Violence against Women in Canada, in memory of the murdered young women. They died for no other reason than the fact that they were women.

The Dalit woman is the doubly or even thrice oppressed in Indian society. She has been called "the dust of the dust."[2] Dalit women are ground to dust by the weight of an oppressive patriarchal caste hierarchy in India—a religiously sanctioned indigenous system that has considered Dalits as the "outcastes" in Indian society. In 2015, in Malpara village near the Taj Mahal, in Agra, an unnamed Dalit woman was raped, dismembered, and her body was burnt to cover up the evidence. While the report[3] does not reveal why this was her fate—as in other cases, one can only conjecture that she must have broken some upper-caste law; polluted the supposedly common well by drawing water from it; or perhaps had the gumption to cross by the landlord's house, thus breaking the unofficial but strongly enforced apartheid-like laws that govern the movement of Dalits in many parts of India. It could also have been a way to teach a lesson to her people for having the courage to speak up; it could be because she dared to fall in love with a man of an upper caste; or simply because the group of upper-caste men wanted to show their power or have some fun. As in such cases, the village headman and others tried to prevent the woman's family from approaching the police by burning her mutilated body—so that all evidence was burnt with her. The police promised action, some arrests were made—but it is common knowledge that the culprits will soon be free. Those with privilege escape punishment all too often, especially when the victim is a woman and a Dalit woman at that. There are frequent reports of the rape and abuse of Dalit women and girls at the hands of landlords, managers, and their masters who they serve. Any upper-caste man or woman possessing authority over Dalits can hold Dalits at ransom, using threats of violence and other forms of pressure. Privilege, power and wealth remain largely in the hands of a minority of upper-caste men in India till today.

ECUMENICAL RESPONSE TO THE VIOLENCE

We live in "a world of contextual violence and episodic justice," as the feminist theologian Mary Hunt once described it.[4] This analysis has framed the WCC's responses over the last few decades. The role of the UN in repeatedly trying to persuade governments and societies to recognize the seriousness of the crimes against women has played a pivotal role in the WCC's own responses.

I quote some hard facts from UN sources which have been updated in August 2017. The United Nations Development Fund for Women, for instance, has estimated that globally at least one of every three women will be beaten, raped, or otherwise abused during her lifetime.[5] The World Health Organization has warned that, "Sexual violence is a pervasive global health and human rights problem. In some countries, approximately one in four women and girls over age fifteen may experience sexual violence by an intimate partner at some point in their lives, and rates of sexual abuse by non-partners range from one to twelve percent over the course of a woman's lifetime."[6] Evidence suggests that certain conditions, under which women live—such as their sexual orientation, disability status or ethnicity, and some contextual factors, such as humanitarian crises, including conflict and post-conflict situations—may increase women's vulnerability to violence. In 2014, 23 percent of LBGTQI women interviewed in Europe indicated having experienced physical and/or sexual violence by both male and female non-partner perpetrators, compared with 5 percent of heterosexual women.[7] In a survey of 3,706 primary schoolchildren from Uganda, 24 percent of eleven to fourteen year-old girls with disabilities reported sexual violence at school, compared to 12 percent of non-disabled girls.[8] Behind these cold statistics are the faces of women and girls, scarred and humiliated, beaten into submission, their bodies broken in times of conflict and of peace.

The ecumenical movement and women in the churches welcomed the launch of a global campaign entitled "16 Days of Activism Against Gender-Based Violence" in 1991 by the Centre for Women's Global Leadership (CWGL), at Rutgers University in the US.[9] Since its launch, the "16 day campaign" has been organized globally, every year from November 25, the International Day for the Elimination of Violence against Women, till December 10, UN's Human Rights Day. It officially includes December 6, that marks Canada's National Day of Remembrance of the Montreal massacre. More than 3,700 organizations from approximately 164 countries participated in the campaign in 2017. The 16-day campaign inspires many local actions, as women take it as an opportunity to highlight forms of violence in their own contexts.

The WCC's proclamation of a *Decade to Overcome Violence (DOV) (2001-2010)* was also welcomed by women, as there was a concern about the increasing violence not only between and within nations; but also, in and within societies; the church; and in the family. With the strong support and engagement of women in the churches all over the world, several programs were initiated in the context of the DOV to sharpen the possibility to re-focus attention on violence against women and girls. The WCC women's program set up a project office in Edinburgh, UK focusing on Overcoming Violence against Women with Leslie Orr Macdonald, Helen Hood and Penny Stuart giving leadership. As the brochure of the project announced:

> The churches are called to join with others in responding to this global crisis (violence against women) with wisdom and courage, justice and compassion, in our theology and worship, in our practice, policies and pastoral care, in our prophetic witness to the vision of God's promised community. The WCC Decade to Overcome Violence (DOV) 2001– 2010, offers a creative framework for cooperation, as we move, in solidarity with all women, to accountability. In recent years, some churches, communions and networks have begun to respond with good practice and procedures. But so much more remains to be done if our churches are truly to become sanctuaries of courage for all God's people.

Women everywhere have broken their silence to tell their stories, share their suffering, and declare their right to live with safety, dignity, respect and love. The Living Letters report on visits to most of WCC member churches observed: "We are convinced that violence against women is not only being more openly reported . . .but it is also escalating." Women who have experienced violence within the church have spoken out with courage and have called the global Christian community to account.

The office collected together and published a selection of the "good practices" of churches around the world in dealing with violence against women.[10] Additionally, there was a wealth of resources collected—statements, plans of action, church level and national level campaigns, and worship materials that were collected, filed and handed over to the WCC archives.

In 2004, a campaign entitled, *"On the Wings of a Dove"*[11] was initiated by the WCC, to directly address the churches, calling on them to participate in the 16 Days campaign during the season of Advent that year. Advent is a season of anticipation, when the church prepares for the incarnation of God's peace in the world. The campaign aimed at engaging the churches in developing pastoral and practical responses and actions to overcome violence against women. It recognizes the potential of world religions to unmask the many forms of violence against women and children prevalent in family, in religious institutions and in society. Women's organizations related to the churches, ecumenical groups and others started many creative initiatives to deal with violence against women and girls. One such initiative was the Tamar Campaign against Gender Based Violence which was announced in Africa by the Fellowship of Christian Councils and Churches in the region of the Great Lakes and Horn of Africa. As the web-site of this campaign announced,

> The church is uniquely placed to play a decisive role in the prevention and elimination of the different forms of violence against women and children. It has the clout and capacity to minister to the needs of those who have been abused as well as those who are perpetrators. The church can provide opportunities for healing for victims, for example, by providing emotional and spiritual support, counseling, and shelter. This would complement the efforts of hospitals, civil society organizations, and the police. It can also provide sanctions and deterrent

measures for perpetrators, for example, by holding them accountable for their deeds, and through counseling. The church can play a proactive role through its preaching and teaching about the evil of gender-based violence, thereby setting standards for societal values that protect women and girls.[12]

As described in an earlier chapter of this book, at the midpoint of the Ecumenical Decade of the Churches in Solidarity with Women, issues requiring focused attention from the churches were identified and of these, the increasing and widespread violence against women was made a priority by women all over the world. In the years before the Churches' Decade, women's movements all over the world had been actively demanding responses from their governments and communities to incidents of violence against women—it was time for the churches to be more proactive and join these efforts and start some of their own.

While the forms of violence and intensity of violence may vary from context to context—the fact remains that regrettably, no society can yet claim that women and children live in a violence free environment. Women conclude that violence is functional—to keep systems of domination in place, whether it be in the context of economic globalization, or of social and cultural structures such as race, caste or sexual orientation; or even of ecclesial structures. Violence is not a symptom of a dysfunctional society—it is so "normal" that many do not react to it any longer! Violence against women has been analyzed from the perspective of three, inter-linked sets of general societal relations: relationships of power (whether at the physical, material, emotional, sexual or psychological levels—who owns, controls, decides); relationships of production (who controls and benefits from production and reproduction of labor/work); and, relationships of distribution (who has access to what resources, who decides this and who has ultimate control over them). Many women experience cross-cutting, triple oppression—race/caste/ethnicity; economic; and, socio-cultural/patriarchal.[13] This nexus of layers of power exists in all our societies in different permutations and combinations. Violence against women is complex and linked with other violent power relations—it can only be addressed in a holistic way, as structures of injustice intertwine and sustain the increasingly cruel forms of violence. Yet, women have persisted in their faith and courageous resistance.

Ecumenical team visits to member churches have become a regular methodology of solidarity that the WCC has organized over the past decades as an alternative method of ecumenical relationship building. In the context of the Decade of the Churches in Solidarity with Women, there were the "Living Letters" visits to the churches described earlier in this book. Additionally, a series of "women to women" solidarity visits were also organized to women in conflict/war situations—Serbia and Croatia, Sierra Leone, former East Timor, Pakistan, Sri Lanka, the Philippines, the Sudan, Rwanda and Kenya were some of the countries visited. The focus of these visits was to provide a space for women in conflict situations to share with women from other parts of the world, first-hand experiences of the extent of violence and deprivation they face in a context of conflict; being caught between warring groups. But, in many places the women also shared stories of resistance and of their attempts to broker peace wherever possible. In not only countries such as Sierra Leone, Angola and Somalia, but also in Israel/Palestine, women have refused to follow what is the politically correct formula and have reached out to women from the so called "enemy" ranks, and women of all sides of the conflict have together marched for peace and demanded an end of hostilities. These visits exposed the way women's bodies are used as a weapon of war—in almost every report of war or conflict a sub-text proclaims, "and many women were raped." Women share heart-rending experiences of violence and sometimes rape, caused by the conflict—when they become pawns in the hands of "the enemy" in the conflict. But then, they very often also share their personal stories of violence in their own homes—women are unsafe everywhere! The context of political/military conflict aggravates the violence they experience in their homes.

Sierra Leone

Braving an explosive and ongoing civil war, a "women to women" visit was organized to Sierra Leone in November 1999. "There is deep despair and hopelessness. But we will not allow it to pull us down,'" the women told the visiting team. The team, composed of representatives of the WCC, the World YWCA, the Lutheran World Federation, and the All Africa Conference of Churches visited several initiatives of women; who had been organizing to meet the needs of their people in different ways, an example being a center for teenage mothers— children who had been raped.

Sierra Leone's nine-year civil war has displaced a quarter of its 4.2 million population and has killed tens of thousands. Human Rights Watch had called it an "unspeakably brutal"[14] war, reporting numerous cases of civilians whose limbs were amputated, children kidnapped, and women raped. Women have suffered the loss of family members, destruction of their homes and frequent displacement. The number of peace-keeping troops with the United Nations Mission to Sierra Leone (UNAMSIL) had grown from 6000 to 13,000 when we visited that country in 1999. The delegation met with Oluyemi Adeniji, the then special envoy to the UNAMSIL, who appreciated the WCC's contributions in setting international standards for conduct in times of conflict and war. He admitted that it was difficult to protect women and children.

The women told us that UN peace keepers had also been raping women—but when we asked officials, no one would confirm this. Only later we read that rebels, government troops and UN peacekeepers were all guilty of raping women on a systematic scale throughout Sierra Leone's brutal civil war. Peter Takirambudde, the head of the Human Rights Watch's Africa division, spoke of the devastating impact of the rape of women and girls. A 75-page report, "We'll Kill You If You Cry," of Africa's Human Rights Watch makes for harrowing reading, with accounts of children being forced to rape grandmothers, fathers made to watch daughters being raped and other instances of serious sexual assault.[15]

The leader of church women at that time in Sierra Leone, Boi Jenneh Jalloh, had come to Geneva to the WCC to appeal to us to not forget the women of Sierra Leone—it was this that convinced us to initiate the "women to women solidarity visits"—and that women in conflict situations need the support of the international community of women. Boi Jenneh met us at the airport and when driving us into town, organized for me to be alone with her in her car. I expected her to give more information on our itinerary and other logistical details—but in fact she just broke down and shared with me (a woman she had almost just met) her personal story of just how much she and her family have been affected by the context in which they live. It moved me tremendously that this woman of power who was so ably leading the women could show her vulnerable side to me even as the sound of gun shots reverberated around us during our drive and throughout the visit. We never spoke of this again—she went on with the business of organizing our visit and taking care of our every need. I have never forgotten her and her amazing spirit.

Sudan

It was a sense of deep hope that peace is coming that we as a team encountered, when we visited Khartoum and nearby Medani in early 2002. The World Council of Churches/All Africa Conference of Churches "women to women solidarity visit" was organized to Khartoum. Once again, we saw that it is women who have acted resolutely to move for peace and to sustain the life of their communities. The women of the Sudan called for the continuing support of the international community as they engage now in efforts for healing and reconciliation, and of reconstructing their lives and those of their communities. The women fear that donor fatigue threatens to abandon them in their hour of need.

Our trip to the Sudan was organized by Joy Kwaje Eluzai—one of the most dynamic women I have ever met. She then worked with the Sudan Council of Churches, heading its women's program but even then, we knew she was destined for political greatness—she was passionate about political freedom for her people in South Sudan. In 2011, South Sudan became a free nation but has since, continuously had to deal with internal conflicts. Joy became a Member of Parliament representing Juba in the South Sudan government—she is a member of the critically important Parliamentary Committee for Economy, Development and Finance in a country still in its infancy. In an interview, I heard that same upbeat and hopeful voice about the future of South Sudan that we had heard when we met her in Khartoum. This strong Christian woman makes all women proud as she contributes to carving out of the future of her fledgling nation.

When we were there, "Peace and Unity" flags dotted the streets of Khartoum—it was the fifteenth anniversary of the coming to power (by a coup) of the present government. Everything was closed for three days and there was heightened security. But, it was also an attempt of the government to impress the then Secretary General of the UN, Dr. Kofi Annan and the former US Secretary of State, Colin Powell, who were visiting Khartoum at that time. However, the message of the ruling party to the US was clear—a poster announced, "We can solve our problems on our own. America, leave us alone."

Twenty-one years of war have left deep scars on the psyche of this nation. Women, we observed, were hesitant to speak of the various forms of violence they have experienced and continue to endure. Darfur has once again shown how rape of women has been systematic, intentional, and has been used as a weapon of war and of ethnic cleansing. Government-backed militia, the *Jenjaweed,* has terrorized the peoples of Darfur forcing them out of their lands.

We were able to speak to women who do not normally get a chance to tell their stories. Most of the women in the Omdurman prison, which we visited, are internally displaced women of African background, from the South of the country. They are in prison for petty crimes such as brewing of a local alcoholic drink. The warden, in conversation with us, acknowledged that "the majority of the 823 women inmates in that overcrowded and filthy prison were there not because they were wicked, but because of their poverty which drives them to find means for themselves and their children to survive."

The women in the desolate Joborona, an Internally Displaced Persons (IDP) camp, shared with us stories of desperation. Ironically, the word *Joborona* in Arabic literally means, "we have been forced." Many of these women have been repeatedly forced out of their homes only to find their houses demolished to make way for city planning and private housing colonies. Most of the people had just made a life for themselves and have built simple houses, when the government authorities bulldozed their houses to the ground and forced them back into make-shift houses made of cardboard boxes and plastic sheets.

We were made aware of the plight of the children of the Sudan—those who have been inducted as child soldiers and "camp followers" (Children who are abducted and used either for sexual purposes or to do domestic chores for the militia). Thousands of children continue to live in a context of violence and insecurity—driven into the streets, orphaned or left to fend for their own survival by poverty stricken single mothers who find themselves in prison for petty crimes.

Regardless of these stories of suffering, we came away with a tremendous sense of hope for the future of Sudan. Even amid state-sponsored attempts at "Arabization" and "Islamization" of the whole society, the church stands strong in its faith and commitment to its Christian identity and responsibility to its people. The women through their deep spirituality expressed in their prayers, songs, and dances, that their profound faith has been the sustaining force throughout the war and their displacement.

A 750-page report issued by Human Rights Watch, entitled "Sudan, Oil and Human Rights,"[16] points out how foreign oil companies have been complicit in major human rights violations committed by the Sudanese government against the indigenous peoples in the oil-drilling regions of the country. Much of the government's earnings from the selling of the oil have been used to buy advanced military weapons. According to the report, issued in November 2003, Sudan earned US\$ 580 million from oil in 2001, and used 250 million to buy helicopters, fixed wing aircraft and other weapons. The government not only used the roads, bridges and airfields built by the oil companies to transport the oil, but also to launch attacks on civilians in the western upper Nile State and the Nuba mountain region, where oil is found in plenty. The government has followed a "scorched earth" policy, to drive out civilians from that part of the country by burning their villages and killing the men, so that the land can be occupied, and the oil exploited. History is repeating itself in the Darfur region which too, analysts point out, is a struggle for the yet untapped oil and mineral rich West Sudan.

The Human Rights Watch report charges that the oil companies that have invested in the South all tended to turn a blind eye to government attacks on civilian targets, including the bombing of hospitals, churches, relief centers and schools. Despite these facts being systematically brought to their attention, they continued their operations undeterred. Relief and church organizations active in the South, human rights NGOs and even UN envoys have been reporting on the government sponsored devastation that had intensified since the oil exploration had begun. According to Human Rights Watch, none of the firms had conceded the abuses that had taken place, let alone provided compensation to the 100,000 indigenous peoples forcibly displaced by the Sudanese army and its allied militia to make way for the companies to operate. In fact, the companies denied these allegations.[17] Many of the displaced now live as the millions in internally displaced people's camps in and around Khartoum, in squalor and misery.

Kenya

"What is it the major challenge to you today?" was the question asked to her. "Men," was the response given by a woman at an internally displaced people's camp site near Limuru, Kenya in January 2008. She was responding to a question posed to her by one of our team, expecting her to respond by sharing the fear in which they lived in the camp always in the shadow of possible attacks from gangs of other ethnic groups. But, she was speaking of the men of her own ethnicity—they had all been crammed into small living spaces and she told us that sexual attacks were common even within the so-called safety of the refugee camps. The context was the unprecedented violence that followed the presidential elections, in a normally peaceful Kenya. On December 27, 2007, the contested poll results were announced and this triggered off brutal and violent attacks because of ethnic rivalry—some 1,000 people had been killed and 30,000 had to flee from their homes. The WCC's visit to Kenya, just one month after the violence erupted, witnessed the continuing attacks and we heard the story of a shattered people.

"According to the Kenyan police crime records, 876 cases of rape and 1,984 of defilement were reported in Kenya between December 27, 2007 and February 29, 2008. The Nairobi Women's Hospital gender violence recovery center treated 443 survivors of sexual and gender-based violence, 80 per cent of which were rape or defilement cases. Between January and March 2008, the hospital and its partner health institutions received at least 900 cases of sexual violence."[18] The figures speak for themselves—rape and sexual abuse of women and children (and some men) go hand in hand with any form of conflict.

These are the reported cases, these are the brutal crimes perpetrated particularly against women and children, to teach a lesson to the men in the so called "enemy" camps of a conflict. What often goes unreported is the atmosphere of violence that penetrates the life of communities, further endangering the lives of women. The violence seems to get aggravated. Women are not safe in times of conflict—not even from so called "peace-keeping" forces; not even from the men of their own communities and homes—there is no place to hide and protect themselves.

Syria

The World Council of Churches women's program had one of its major meetings of Orthodox Christian women in Damascus, Syria in 1996. Over the years, the WCC has condemned the inhuman and bloody war in this region. In a letter, the General Secretary of the WCC wrote to the churches in Syria and around the world:

> Our hearts and prayers are with all those in Syria who are suffering from war and violence, from injustices and oppression, and from being forgotten by the international community. We ask God to comfort all those who have lost their beloved ones. We affirm that we stand in solidarity with the suffering people of Syria and hope that their aspirations for freedom and human dignity will be reached soon through putting an end to this absurd war and engaging in the political process led by the UN in accordance with relevant UNSC resolutions.[19]

A new report has shed light on the alarming extent to which Syrian internally displaced people (IDPs), specifically women and girls, have for years been subject to sexual exploitation from local men working for the UN and aid organizations, in order to access basic necessities such as food, medicine and shelter. The report, published by a research group, *The Whole of Syria*, expresses deeply disturbing findings on the incidence of gender-based violence among internal refugee communities in Syria. It highlights the "common risk" faced by women and girls of sexual exploitation by humanitarian workers when trying to access aid. The effects of the ongoing conflict; poverty, displacement, and women being head of the household, coupled with gender inequality, have acutely exacerbated the problem of sexual exploitation, according to the report.

Worryingly, unaccompanied girls, or those living in a female-headed household—which is common in IDP communities—are perceived to be highest at risk from this type of exploitation, the report states.

> British aid worker Danielle Spencer has shared her experience of sexual exploitation of female IDPs—and how it has been ignored throughout the seven-year conflict—in a video for the *BBC*. She explains how local Syrian men, working on behalf of the UN and other humanitarian agencies, exchanged aid for sex. "Women and girls need to be protected when they are trying to receive food, and soap, and basic items to live. The last thing you need is a man who you're supposed to trust and receive aid from then asking you to have sex with him and withholding that aid from you," Spencer said. "The UN and the system as it currently stands have chosen for women's bodies to be sacrificed. Somewhere, there has been a decision made that it is okay for women's bodies to continue to be used, abused, violated, in order for aid to be delivered to a larger group of people," she added.[20]
>
> The Syrian conflict began when the Baath regime, in power since 1963 and led by President Bashar al-Assad, responded with military force to peaceful protests for democratic reforms during the Arab Spring wave of uprisings, triggering an armed rebellion fueled by mass defections from the Syrian army. According to independent monitors, hundreds of thousands of civilians have been killed in the war, mostly by the regime and its powerful allies, and millions have been displaced both inside and outside of Syria. The brutal tactics pursued mainly by the regime, which have included the use of chemical weapons, sieges, mass executions and torture against civilians have led to war crimes investigations.[21]

STREAMS OF GRACE—GLIMPSES OF SOLIDARITY

Fortunately, the churches have, over the years, made efforts to speak out and act to overcome violence against women.[22] A major contribution was made through the Ecumenical Decade of the Churches in Solidarity with Women (1988-1998).

Throughout the Decade, the many forms of violence that women experience were exposed. Many methodologies were used to tackle the seriousness of the issue. A series of regional gatherings of women (which included men in some instances) focused on identifying the issues specific to each continent—Asia, Africa, Latin America, North America, the Pacific, Europe and the Middle East had such gatherings.[23]

The Bali Declaration (1993) of Asian women states,

> The family along with the state today has sought to control women through rigid definitions of sexuality; and appropriate for itself reproductive rights and control over the body. Violence and subjugation have been woven into institutionalized forms of religion whose patriarchal tenets have marginalized and domesticated the female and the feminine, shackling her and legitimizing violence against her. Social and legal codes of justice have either been blind to crimes against women, like wife battering and prostitution that have in fact received tacit social approval; or have seen violations like sexual assault and rape as acts of individual aberration and deviance and has even rendered some totally invisible as in the case of homosexuality.[24]

Women of Latin America in their San Jose Declaration (1993) defined violence as more than all the physical forms in which it manifests itself—they named ecclesial forms of exclusion too as violence.

> When women's ministerial gifts are not respected and rather tasks are imposed that are appropriate to women's gender, when the church promotes doctrines, traditions and patriarchal and culturally bound structures that marginalize women; and especially when pastors, priests, and church leaders are perpetrators of sexual abuse.[25]

African women in their Nyeri statement (1994) concluded that,

> Women are subjected to psychological pain, disease and death while the people of God look on silently. The time to act is now. Men and women who see this as a trivial issue are clearly disobeying God's call and choosing to be partners with agents of death. God still calls "Who shall I send, and who will go for us?" It is imperative for us to respond, "Here we go, send us!"[26]

113

The Ballycastle Declaration (1994) of European women set out their vision:

> We look for a world where conflicts are resolved without violence
> Where power is found in the enabling strength of solidarity
> And not in domination legitimized by force and fear.
> We look for a world where all people have the space
> To live and grow in dignity
> Where all women can discern their worth and competence
> Where we experience the liberating power of justice and love.[27]

Women of the Middle East, in their Ayia Napa Declaration (1995) spoke together in the first person:

> My voice emerges from a region that has a long history replete with intense struggle and constant wars . . . My oppressors are many: first, my vulnerability and ignorance that I have been carrying all along and which I will put off today; second, my society which made me believe that my body is a curse . . . They muzzle my mouth if I cry.
>
> I am searching for a world that hears my silent voice, appreciates me for what I am, encourages and respects my femininity and motherhood genuinely . . . . In this manner I can promote peace that Jesus Christ calls for in the area which witnessed his birth.[28]

Women of the Pacific, in their Apia Declaration, (1996) "Tofamamao: No More Violence in Paradise," said,

> Strengthened and encouraged by each other and the unconditional love of God, we reached out to each other and shared our painful experiences and stories of the violence against women throughout the Pacific Islands . . . .We are confronted with the knowledge that our cultures have been used as justification for violence against women. The church is the *alia* (canoe) of the gospel. For the *alia* to move forward, there must be equal partnership and participation between all who are in the *alia*. This will mean that all will take up their oars and row in harmony. If some of the members within the *alia* row faster and stronger than others, the *alia* will either capsize or not move at all . . . . We call on the churches to stand in solidarity with us . . . . and work together until there is no more violence in paradise.[29]

North American women (from Canada and the US) met in Bolton, Canada (1996). A few sentences from their report:

> We must understand that oppression is a condition of life which has been imposed and enforced on people by dominant groups. Suffering that takes away human dignity is always wrong! A theology of suffering is helpful, if it moves us to recognize injustice and work toward the ending of suffering, toward the upholding of human dignity . . . Language for the Eucharist needs to be that of a banquet, rather than a sacrifice, if abuse survivors are to feel this is truly an occasion for celebration and thanksgiving.[30]

All the regional gatherings did have young women among the participants; however, a special young women's Festival was held in Suva, Fiji in 1994 which brought together sixty women (including a few young men) from forty nations. In their statement entitled, "We are Worthy: Young Women Demand a Violence Free World...Now!" they said,

> We envision a church that is more concerned with the gospel than with the status quo. We envision a church that will influence cultures rather than be influenced by patriarchal cultures of our societies. We envision a church that not only stands behind women, but beside women recognizing our worth and dignity. We envision a church that is truly in solidarity with women.[31]

I have quoted from each of the regional meetings and from the young women to underline just how important this issue has been to women; and the role the WCC has played in providing a safe ecumenical space for women to speak about this and to design their own responses for their churches and communities. As mentioned earlier, most of this series of meetings were for women alone; tragically in the meetings where men were invited there was some tension—with men on occasion telling women what they should think or do; or even ridiculing the women; or in one instance, speaking of rape in an offensive way, causing distress to the women.

It was fitting therefore that the process concluded with a global gathering of men and women in 1997—theologians, pastors, lay leaders and church administrators—entitled, "Together with Courage: Women and Men Living without Violence against Women." The men and women who gathered in Geneva for this discussion read all the regional reports and based on that, explored the roots of the increasing violence against women. They said it is founded in the "increasing globalization of world markets and the concurrent exclusion of large sections of the population"; "the inequality of power relations between women and men even within the life of the churches"; "ecclesiastical and clergy power"; "the silence of the churches"; "the lack of accountability in the church"; "a culture of impunity"; and "a biased reading of the Bible."[32] They said together,

> In contexts where women's bodies are made into objects and commodities, women are violated, the image of God is defiled and God's whole creation is distorted. We challenge the churches to reflect further on how to affirm our bodies and sexuality as gifts from God to be cherished and nurtured as temples of the Holy Spirit and we seek full commitment to women's right to make their own responsible choices.[33]

WHEN THE ECUMENICAL DECADE ENDED

As the final report of the Living Letters visits quoted earlier in this book says,

> Although every church is against violence in principle, our visits unhappily confirmed that not all are opposed to it in practice. The churches tend to let violent men go free and at the same time prevent women from speaking out against the violence . . . the failure of the churches to publicly condemn such violence and state clearly that it is against the teachings of Christ appeared with distressing regularity . . . . In many places we encountered theological justification for the violence against women and misinterpretations of man-woman relations in the Bible.[34]

The WCC, through all its work in this period, opened up discussions on domestic violence; on the so called "comfort women" to Japanese soldiers in war camps during the Second World War (a form of abuse that continues in other conflicts); honor killings of women by their own families when they dare to make alliances with men of another religion (or in the case of South Asia, with men of another caste group); the use of cultural practices to discriminate against women; prostitution and trafficking in women and children; pornography and the objectifying of

116

women and children; denigrating images of women in media, and other similar concerns.

As the report of the Living Letters states,

> We met them during our journey
> endless numbers of women
> Who were weeping.
> > But nobody asked them, why they wept
> > not even the church
> > that has promised
> > to follow the way of Jesus.
> We met these women
> > in church offices and shelters
> > in Christian homes and church gatherings
> women whose pain is hidden, yet so real
> > invisible, forgotten, ignored women
> > women who survived
> > and those whose story remains that of victims
> women whose bruises were made by a man of their church
> > and whose suffering
> > is justified by their loyalty to their church
> > and whose lips are kept locked
> > by the advice of a priest.
> We met these women
> > in each country and each church.
> We understood that
> > violence against women
> > exists in our very midst.

Irja Askola (1997)

It was no wonder then that the Decade Festival held in Harare, Zimbabwe at the end of the Decade in 1998 had a special hearing to acknowledge the violence women experience in the context of the churches themselves. Beautifully choreographed by Irja Askola,[35] this half day event included a Canadian clergy woman who spoke of being sexually abused as a child by her priest father; a woman from Papua New Guinea who said she was in a violently abusive marriage for six years and sought an annulment which she was not granted by the church—she finally left the abusive husband for another caring man. Twenty-two years later, the church had taken no action and she was denied the sacraments after that. Not all the stories described physical violence. A clergy woman from Aotearoa-New Zealand spoke of how she was forced to resign from her position as the coordinator of the education ministry of the church because her supervisors perceived her as a trouble-maker. When she asked her church to evaluate why she had been forced out, her bishop interpreted her request as a "personal attack." Her ministry license was not renewed. "To those who look at me, the metaphorical bruises do not show," the woman said. "Yet from the inside the 'bruises' have become disabling. The face of the institution is still smiling benevolently; the words from its painted mouth are still sweet."[36] Ada Maria Isasi-Diaz, a *mujerista* theologian from the US, spoke of the violence done to women-centered theologies and women theologians with these powerful words:

> Our voices are not heard, what we say is not considered important; women are silenced when we are not listened to, when we are ignored. Some might think that because we get books published we are heard . . . but our reflections/explanations of what we believe are not valued . . . because we are not considered capable of explaining our beliefs. We are considered only capable of repeating what the male theologians and church officials say. We are considered only capable of believing what others tell us we should believe.

The hearing on violence against women in the church at the Festival opened with a liturgical ceremony in which nine women from all regions of the world carried vessels of water representing women's tears and poured the water into a large bowl placed on the altar. "I bring the tears of women (from my region), of those who survived and those who never made it," said each woman. "Our tears as victims of war and internal conflicts. Our tears as women whose story was never told. Our tears as women, struggling to survive because of national debts and global economic control." Each of the nine women said words that identified the issues of violence as pertinent to their own context. Chung Hyun-Kyung, the Korean feminist theologian closed the session with a healing action in the Shaman tradition—leading the Festival from the crucifixion to resurrection focusing on the healing power women bring to each other.

During the hearing, the then General Secretary of the WCC, Konrad Raiser—the only man on the podium—declared that the church "should not cover up the sickness anymore. My final commitment is to work for and encourage a community of women and men where the sin of violence against women can be confessed and the healing power of forgiveness can be experienced."[37]

In all the work of the past decades, men have been invited as partners with the understanding of the church as a community of women and men. Positive masculinities have been affirmed and the program has engaged men in the conversation. WCC worked with and encouraged the work of the World Communion of Reformed Churches "in the production of a church manual for the promotion of positive masculinities to dismantle the paradigm of power that is prevalent in the world."[38] The Manual was designed for congregations and other communities to use, and has been used in many parts of the world, to help communities to reconstruct masculinities, "which are not based on competitiveness, power, control, violence and repression of emotions."[39]

IDENTIFYING THE THEOLOGICAL AND ETHICAL CHALLENGES THAT NEED TO BE ADDRESSED[40]

Given the rich history of engagement and active solidarity, the question to be asked is what the churches can do yet. Thus far, it is women who have been exploring the theological questions to expose both the causes of violence and in seeking answers. The theological foundations for finding peace with justice for women is key, as the theology that the church teaches women has too often been at the source of the silence of women in violent situations. At the special hearing during the Decade Festival on violence against women in the church, referred to earlier, Ada Maria Isasi-Diaz reminded the gathered women and men that male dominated church structures abuse women by not taking seriously their theology or their spiritual gifts. "Women need to understand that God can be understood through women's experience. Women's theologies simply reclaim that as women we are made in the image of God."[41]

The biblical affirmation "made in God's image" has been the core message giving women the courage to recognize themselves not as victims but as survivors. Feminist theologians have claimed that since we are made in the image of God, we will resist all forms of violence against our bodies that are akin to the Body of God. Any form of violence against women is an aggression against the Body of God. Yet, in spite of this foundational Christian teaching, women have themselves so often silently acquiesced to the worst forms of abuse. Women's bodies have been the site of possession, conquest and control because of the dominant patriarchal cultures and the values in all our societies.

Mercy Amba Oduyoye, theologian from Ghana, writes,

> In the search for liberating hermeneutics, many women have claimed the biblical affirmation of our being created "in the image of God" both for the promotion of women's self-worth and self-esteem and to protest dehumanization by others . . . . If one is in the image of God, then one is expected to practice the hospitality, compassion and justice that characterize God.[42]

Oduyoye continues, this "must begin with women learning to be hospitable to themselves, to not allow the invasion of their bodies, gifts from God, temple of God and inescapable part of our humanity."[43]

Christian anthropology has been the source of much of the inferiority heaped on women—of making the female body an obstacle to the fullness of woman's humanness in the hierarchy of creation. The popular understanding continues to be that woman was created less than man. A traditional theology of dualism has not only divided the male and the female but has also divided the body from the divine and has placed the divine somewhere outside our lives and everyday experiences. As Oduyoye explains,

> An element that is missing from traditional Christian anthropology is a positive appropriation of our embodiment. The necessity of facing the issue of human sexuality as an integral part of our humanness and a gift from God is a specific contribution of women theologians to religious anthropology. The fear of our bodies has made it difficult to accept the integrity of our

being and led to the separation of our make up into material and spiritual, body and soul/spirit/mind.[44]

Nancy Cardoso Pereira, the Brazilian feminist theologian, has developed what Latin American women define as "a body hermeneutic"—a new theological methodology. This is not just a new way of doing theology but is seen as the starting point for constructing knowledge. Writing on behalf of a group of women biblical scholars in Latin America, Nancy Cardoso-Pereira writes,

> Reading the passion and resurrection of Jesus with the lacerated bodies of Latin America in mind requires us to contemplate the raped bodies of men and women, boys and girls, and to feel the urgent need for resurrection of these bodies now. The recreation of the body as a place of sacred revelation means accepting and affirming the liberating dynamics of enjoyment, pleasure without shame, without the limits imposed by shame, stereotypes and oppressive censorship.[45]

Asian theologians such as Hyun Kyung Chung from Korea, Kwok Pui Lan from Hong Kong, and Evangeline Anderson-Rajkumar, Dalit womanist theologian from India, have made important contributions to a theology of "embodiment" that challenges the abuse of the female body in any way. Sexuality is a taboo topic in the church and has been shrouded in silence and the church has remained unable to address the many forms of sexual violence against women, even that which occurs right in the heart of the church—clergy sexual abuse and pedophilia continue till today in all parts of the world. They remain as "embarrassing" and hidden secrets and are a sign of the corruption of ecclesial power and authority.

"Christology, Atonement, Forgiveness and Healing": These are perhaps the most difficult of the themes that women have addressed as we seek to find healing. Unfortunately, some in the churches have used the doctrines of the cross and of atonement to silence women. "Every time I beat my wife she should thank me, because she is one step closer to salvation," said a church leader to the team that was visiting his church in the context of the Ecumenical Decade of the Churches in Solidarity with Women. The cross has been the strongest symbol of Christ's identification as co-sufferer with the oppressed. However, to women, its meaning has been distorted by a theology of sacrifice and suffering that the churches teach. A sacrificial lifestyle and a commitment to die for the other are indeed Christ-like qualities that women would emulate, if it would lead to the liberation of themselves, their families and their communities. It is a well-known fact that women would give up everything, their own dreams and aspirations, for the sake of their families, especially for their children. Often this is a voluntary act, a conscious decision that some women make. However, it is equally true that because of this, women have borne pain and hurt for centuries, silently many times, standing on the threshold of a violent death in the hands of the man they live with, having no other alternative; or socialized into believing that this is their lot—they have no choice but to bear it all in silence. Alternatively, it could be the experience of restrictions of time, space and movement that is imposed on women through strict mores and values of a patriarchal world order.

To Delores Williams, "Jesus did not come to die for humankind; Jesus came to live for humankind. Thus, it is Jesus' life and his ministerial vision that redeem humans."[46] Muriel Orevillo-Montenegro from the Philippines writes, "I (also) found Christ among women and men, who live out a loving, life-giving, and life-sustaining praxis. This liberated Christ continues to call everyone to follow the way that leads to the fullness of life for all."[47]

Oduyoye claims that the problem lies in the "collusion of the church" with the various forms of oppression of women. To her, "Christian discipleship is crucial" in dealing with these issues.

> If unmerited suffering is redemptive, then in a community of women and men travelling with the suffering Christ, all need to share that suffering. Do not the Beatitudes apply to men? Christian women should challenge the theology, Christology and anthropology that do violence to women's humanity.[48]

The letter from the Decade Festival to the churches at the Eighth Assembly, denounced violence against women as "sin" and the churches were called to repent for their participation in the violence. The understanding of sin is further unraveled by women theologians. The alienation from each other due to violence must be the starting point for the interpretation of sin, according to Rosemary Radford Ruether. She is critical of the church, which has reduced sin to purely a question of alienation from God.[49] Redemption will come only when there is a healing of relationships between the victim and victimizer and not by an act of divine intervention which does not consider the pain and suffering of the victim.

"Survival and resistance": In the analysis of violence against women, the question of impunity must be addressed. It is this that can free us to explore other theological values such as forgiveness, reconciliation and justice—which are integral parts of any work that can be done in overcoming violence against women. Women and children are most often deliberately made targets of violence, and the perpetrators of violence are too often granted amnesty. To achieve true reconciliation between women and men, impunity given to male perpetrators of crimes needs to be addressed. The essential elements for the healing of wounds and for the restoration of broken social relationships, are the relearning of how to live together in peace and mutual trust, reclaiming historical memory, and learning how to deal with the truth with justice, forgiveness and repentance. In this, the church has a primary role to play.

A world without violence against women is possible—not just a reduction in violence, or creation of the climate for women to learn to tolerate violence but to put an end to the violence. It is a call for the agency as churches and all individual Christians along with all other concerned people, to act with conviction and determination. Women have begun a search for a new paradigm for life that will be more caring of humanity and of creation.

It is appropriate to end this chapter with these powerful voices of women, many from countries mentioned in this book who came together in Geneva in 2002 for a Consultation on "Peace with Justice: Women Speak Out!"

> As we laughed and cried together, we shared numerous stories that spoke of bravery, resolve, determination, wisdom, and deep insight into the true meaning of life in community. Our vision of peace and justice was imbued with continuing resistance to the power of violent patriarchal institutions in eroding our sense of humanity. Our accounts enumerated the several ways in which we are involved in making the visions a reality in our public and private lives. We sought and shared ways in which peace and a full life in communities could be realized for all members of the community; it meant creating models of inclusive community living. We recognized the necessity of

simultaneously challenging patriarchal structures of power and exercising our own individual and collective power at home and in our societies. To that end, we acknowledged the need for immediate cessation of violence in all its forms, a sustained commitment to peace in our homes and nations, and restoration of the dignity, respect, and humanity for women all over the world.[50]

The final chapter of this book will assess what the WCC has achieved in its work with women and will point forward to the future.

ENDNOTES

[1] Rita Nakashima Brock and Rebecca Ann Parker, *Proverbs of Ashes: Violence, Redemptive Suffering, and the Search for What Saves Us* (Massachusetts: Beacon Press, 2001), 9.

[2] Indian society is divided into a four-fold occupation-based and religiously sanctioned form of graded subjugation, called the caste system—with the Brahmins, or the intellectual "priestly caste," at the apex; followed by the Shatriya, or warrior caste, next; and the Vaishya, or the merchant caste, after that; and the Shudra, or working classes, coming last. And then some 25 percent of the population of India are considered "out-castes"—based on the principle of ritual impurity, they are relegated to the most menial and degrading of occupations, considered unclean and polluting. The caste system that is based on privilege has systematically stamped on the rights and dignity of the out-castes. However, the leader of the Dalit Community, Dr. B. R. Ambedkar, who was in fact the main drafter of the Indian constitution, organized his community and gave them the name Dalits—a word which literally means "the broken, the oppressed." Dr. Ambedkar reclaimed this word and infused it with positive meaning, symbolizing the resistance movement of Dalits for justice and

freedom from the bondage of caste oppression. He called Dalit women "the dust of the dust of the dust" as they are the most oppressed in a caste ridden and patriarchal Indian society.

3   In a report by Subhajit Sengupta, entitled "Goons Allegedly Gang rape, Murder Dalit Woman, Cut Her Body into Pieces" in CNN-IBN, July 21, 2015. I include this example to underline that even within the population of women the hierarchy of caste keeps layers of graded subjugation intact; though almost every day reports of rape and abuse of women continue in India—a few years ago dubbed "the rape capital" of the world, accessed June 1, 2017, merionwest.com/2017/05/28/is-india-really-the-rape-capital-of-the-world.

4   Mary Hunt, "Waging War at Home: Christianity and Structural Violence," in *Miriam's Song V,* Priests for Equality (West Hyattsville, MD: Priests for Equality, 1992).

5   United Nations Development Fund for Women, "Not a Minute More: Ending Violence Against Women," , accessed July 4, 2017, http://www.unifem.org/resources.

6   Garcia-Moreno et al. *WHO Multi-Country Study on Women's Health and Domestic Violence Against Women,* World Health Organization, 2008, accessed July 4, 2012, http://www.who.int/gender/violence/who_multicountry_study/en/. See also European Union Agency for Fundamental Rights, *Violence Against Women: An EU-Wide Survey, 2014,* Annex 3, 184-188. A survey by the European Union Agency for Fundamental Rights.

7   See European Union Agency for Fundamental Rights, *Violence Against Women: An EU-Wide Survey,* 2014, Annex 3, 184-188.

8   K. M. Devries et al. Violence against Primary School Children with Disabilities in Uganda: A Cross-Sectional Study, 2014, 6, accessed April 15, 2019, https://www.ncbi.nlm.nih.gov/pubmed/25270531.

9   "The National Union of Students-Union of Students in Ireland (NUS-USI)," accessed April 15, 2019, https://nus-usi.org/2017/11/26/history-of-the-16-days-of-activism-against-gender-violence.

10   *Streams of Grace: A Dossier*, WCC 2005, collated by Helen Stuart, Helen Hood and Lesley Orr. Some examples of "good practice" by individual churches, church groups, ecumenical bodies are recognized as signs of hope in responding to violence against women.

11   "On the Wings of a Dove," accessed on April 15, 2019, http://www.overcomingviolence.org/en/extra/archive/past-campaigns/on-the-wings-of-a-dove-2004.html.

12   "The Tamar Campaign," accessed April 15, 2019, http://www.fecclaha.org/index.php/en/what-we-do/gender-justice/protection-against-gender-based-violence-and-tamar-campaign.

13   "South Africa's Other Epidemic," accessed November 18, 2017, http://www.womensnet.org.za/news/south-africas-other-epidemic-violence-against-women.

14   "Shocking War Crimes in Sierra Leone, New Testimonies on Mutilation, Rape of Civilians," accessed April 15, 2019, https://www.hrw.org/news/1999/06/24/shocking-war-crimes-sierra-leone.

[15] "We'll Kill You if You Cry," accessed April 15, 2019, https://www.hrw.org/report/2003/01/16/well-kill-you-if-you-cry/sexual-violence-sierra-leone-conflict; "A Report of Human Rights Watch, 2003," accessed April 15, 2019, https://www.hrw.org/reports/2003/sierraleone.

[16] "Sudan, Oil and Human Rights": Report of the Human Rights Watch, accessed April 15, 2019, https://www.hrw.org/reports/2003/sudan1103/sudan-print.pdf.

[17] "Oil Sales Lead to Deaths in Sudan," Every Voice Network, Anglican Voices United for Justice, November 25, 2003.

[18] From a report by All Africa.com daily news on the web, "Kenya: Post Election Violence Not Spontaneous," April 2, 2010, accessed July 2, 2010, http://allafrica.com/stories.

[19] Statement on Syria from the General Secretary of the WCC, February 26, 2018, Geneva.

[20] "Sex for Aid," accessed March 3, 2018, https://www.alaraby.co.uk/english/News/2018/2/27/Syrianrefugees-forced-to-exchange-sex-for-aid.

[21] "Sex for Aid," accessed March 3, 2018, https://www.alaraby.co.uk/english/News/2018/2/27/Syrianrefugees-forced-to-exchange-sex-for-aid.

[22] Stuart, Hood and Orr, *Streams of Grace*, WCC, 2005.

[23] *Together with Courage: Women and Men Living without Violence against Women* (1998: WCC, Geneva.)

[24] "The Bali Declaration, Asian Women's Declaration," 1993, Bali, Indonesia. *Together with Courage,* 11.

[25] "The San Jose Declaration, Latin American Women's Declaration," 1993, San Jose, Costa Rica. *Together with Courage,* 18.

[26] "The Nyeri Statement, African Women's Statement," 1994, Nyeri, Kenya. *Together with Courage,* 25.

[27] "The Ballycastle Declaration," European Women's Declaration, Ballycastle, Northern Ireland, 1994, *Together with Courage,* 27.

[28] "The Aiya Napa Declaration, Middle Eastern Women's Declaration," 1995, Ayia Napa, Cyprus. *Together with Courage,* 33.

[29] "Apia Declaration: Tofamamao: No More Violence in Paradise," women from the Pacific, 1996, Apia, Western Samoa, *Together with Courage,* 36-38.

[30] "Report of the North American Regional Meeting on Violence against Women," 1996, Bolton, Ontario, *Together with Courage,* 40-47.

[31] Young Women's Festival, 1994, Suva, Fiji "Message to the Churches," *Together with Courage,* 50-51.

[32] *Together with Courage: Women and Men Living without Violence against Women* (WCC, Geneva, 1998). 5-8.

[33] *Together with Courage,* 7.

[34] *Living Letters: A Report of the Visits to the Churches during the Ecumenical Decade of the Churches in Solidarity with Women* (Geneva: WCC Publications), 1997.

[35] Irja Askola, a Lutheran feminist from Finland, recently retired as Bishop of Helsinki (2010-2017). She was the first female bishop in the Evangelical Lutheran Church of Finland. She was then an executive secretary in the Conference of European Churches which had its headquarters in Geneva and shared an office in the WCC. During her time, there were many forms of co-operative work between the WCC and the Conference of European Churches.

[36] From a Press Release, Ecumenical Decade Festival (No. 2), WCC, November 28, 1998, accessed April 15, 2019, http://www.wcc-coe.org/wcc/assembly/festiv-e.html.

[37] From a Press Release, Ecumenical Decade Festival (No. 2), WCC, November 28, 1998, accessed April 15, 2019, http://www.wcc-coe.org/wcc/assembly/festiv-e.html.

[38] Patricia Sheerattan-Bisnauth and Philip Peacock, *Created in God's Image: From Hegemony to Partnership: A Church Manual on Men as Partners: Promoting Positive Masculinities* (Geneva: World Communion of Reformed Churches and the World Council of Churches, 2010).

[39] Patricia Sheerattan-Bisnauth, Introduction, *Created in God's Image: From Hegemony to Partnership,* 5.

[40] For this section, I have drawn some extracts from a paper titled "Overcoming Violence Against Women: Theological Reflections," that I had presented at a one-day public event organized by the WCC's Project Office on Violence Against Women in the context of the Decade to Overcome Violence, held in Glasgow, Scotland, April 9, 2005.

[41] From a Press Release, Ecumenical Decade Festival (No. 2), WCC, November 28, 1998, accessed April 15, 2019, http://www.wcc-coe.org/wcc/assembly/festiv-e.html.

[42] Mercy Amba Oduyoye, "Spirituality of Resistance and Reconstruction," in *Women Resisting Violence, Spirituality for Life,* eds. Mananzan Mary John, Mercy Amba Oduyoye, Elsa Tamez et al. (New York: Orbis Books, 1995), 170.

[43] Mary Grey, quoting Mercy Amba Oduyoye in *Introducing Feminist Images of God,* Introductions in Feminist Theology (Sheffield, England: Sheffield Academic Press, 2001), 82.

[44] Mercy Amba Oduyoye, *Introducing African Women's Theology* (Sheffield: Sheffield Academic Press, 2001), 69.

[45] Nancy Cordosa-Pereira, *The Ecumenical Review* 54, no. 3 (July 2002): 236.

[46] Delores Williams, "Atonement," in *Dictionary of Feminist Theologies,* eds. Letty M. Russell and J. Shannon Clarkson (Louisville, Kentucky: Westminster John Knox Press, 1996), 18.

[47] Muriel Orevillo-Montenegro, *The Jesus of Asian Women* (Maryknoll, New York: Orbis Books 2006), 194.

[48] Mercy Amba Oduyoye, "Violence against Women: Window on Africa," Voices from the Third World (EATWOT) VIII, no.1 (June 1995): 175. See also Aruna Gnanadason, *No Longer a Secret, The Church and Violence against Women,* Revised ed. (Geneva: RISK Books, World Council of Churches Publication, 1997).

[49] Rosemary Radford Ruether, *Introducing Redemption in Christian Feminism*, Introductions to Feminist Theology (Sheffield: Sheffield Academic Press, 1998), 70.

[50] Consultation on Peace with Justice: Women Speak Out! (March 16-21, 2002, Ecumenical Centre, Geneva, Switzerland). It was jointly organized by the World Council of Churches, Lutheran World Federation, World Alliance of Reformed Churches, and the Conference of European Churches, Geneva. The fifty or so women participants came from Sierra Leone, Liberia, Kenya, Rwanda, South Africa; Jamaica, Trinidad and Tobago, Guyana, Costa Rica, Brazil, Peru, Bolivia, Argentina; Lebanon, Israel; United States of America and Canada; UK, Belgium/ Germany, Yugoslavia, Bosnia-Herzegovina, Serbia, Switzerland; Afghanistan, Taiwan, Sri Lanka, India, Pakistan, Indonesia, Aceh/Indonesia, Japan, Australia; Fiji, Papua New Guinea.

CHAPTER 5

MOVING FORWARD: HOLDING EACH OTHER UP GENTLY

In the Scriptures the Spirit is so often associated with the female gender. She broods like a mother over her young; she sweeps like a wind across the world; she inspires wisdom, like a woman pondering the word; she groans in childbirth, longing for the appearance of a new creation. This is a disturbing Spirit, soaring where she wills, apparently uncontrollable.

Pauline Webb[1]

In this last chapter, I draw together some of my personal observations on events as they unfolded in the sphere of women's participation and work in the WCC and will consider some of the lessons we could learn. We have journeyed together in solidarity as women; and even if there have been a few glitches and even obstacles on the way, we have so much to be grateful for. The WCC and other ecumenical and global Christian organizations have stayed on track in their commitments to women, as we, as women, have been to the churches and the ecumenical movement. Some questions remain, and the agenda is far from being completed with satisfaction. So, where do we go from here?

Throughout this ecumenical journey, there is an awareness of the company of many women all over the world. The list is endless, and it stretches across the world. The stories of women struggling to survive; raising their voices in faith to a God to whom they turn in praise and celebration; or voices raised in protest against injustice and threats to peace for all; refusing to hate the enemy and holding each other tenderly as they try to stand upright. These amazing women and their stories are woven into the history of the ecumenical movement and into the work with women. It has been a journey in search of a round table that will draw all women together into a circle of resistance and hope.

We sat at round tables at the end of the Decade Festival held in 1998 to mark the end of the Decade. Except for the practical need to divide the 2000 or so women who came, into language groups; there was no hierarchy in the seating—no high table for dignitaries or church leaders. Women from the pews sat with women bishops, women working for agencies of the churches, activists, women church workers and evangelists, theologians, ordained women and lay sat together fifteen or so to a table, including some of the men present. All participants got their table number, which was randomly picked, when they registered. The tables were set in the gymnasium of the Belvedere Women's Education college in Harare, decorated by women from the local churches—painstakingly and lovingly, with vases of fresh flowers on colored table cloths with African prints, neatly pinned down. It indeed looked festive as women from all parts of the world slowly filled the hall and searched for their table numbers and sat down and greeted each other. The authorities of the college were surprised at our choice for the venue—they offered us their auditorium, but its fixed tiered seats would not have been conducive for the festive atmosphere created in the gymnasium. Two young local artists, Passmore Makoni and Charles Nyokanhete, decorated the space and the area around it. The huge backdrop painted by these artists hung across one wall—a canvas of a river scene—with the water seemingly flowing right across the hall. On one side of the backdrop, the artists had painted Zimbabwean women carrying pots of water—this provided the perfect setting for the Festival which had the theme of water flowing through its liturgical life prepared to perfection by Lus Marina Campos Garcia, Lutheran pastor from Brazil; and musician/liturgist Lynda Katsuno from the Anglican Church in Canada, along with a team.

The round tables became the space for dialogue and discussion, across cultures and church and denominational contexts, on issues that were difficult at times. At many tables there was attentive listening to each other; earnest words and prayers said together, tears shed, and laughter, at times. Deep friendships were formed as the participants learnt from each other and offered opinions that occasionally sparked controversy. The Decade Festival was a celebration in many ways and roundtables of cross cultural, cross denominational and cross generational conversations were made possible. The WCC learnt from this ecumenical experience and moved to using round tables at its Central Committee meetings to facilitate greater participation among its members.

But that period of ecumenical history around the Festival and the Eighth Assembly to follow in 1998, also exposed that it is not always a smooth ride for women. The faith and hope women have placed on the ecumenical movement was severely tested in Harare. Some of the many women who have served in the governing bodies of the WCC are remembered in this book or reference is made to their contributions. With them, names of eminent women who have served in the WCC secretariat in Geneva can be added—women who have throughout this history kept vigilant, have spoken out when needed; and have ensured WCC's sustained commitment to women. With fortitude, patience, and "subversive" power, women have offered their courageous voices to the movement at every stage.[2] Ably supported by some men, there have been moments when women have had to break all conventions to be heard if change was to come. This has not always been easy, it has even been painful at times, but women have persisted. There was that occasion when the Women's Staff Advisory group led by Ofelia Ortega from Cuba, had to storm into the Staff Leadership Meeting to press for the inclusion of women in all aspects of the Seventh Assembly of the WCC in Canberra—after repeated suggestions were ignored. There were also the continuing efforts to monitor and ensure that women are well represented in decision making bodies, as staff and in all the work of the WCC. Sometimes it has been a disappointing struggle.

One glaring example of this was when we failed to convince the leadership that we ought to have a woman as moderator of the central committee of the WCC for the period after the Eighth Assembly in Harare. The pain and disappointment of women was palpable, because this Assembly followed the end of the Decade; and came right after the Decade Festival in Harare, that had so strongly celebrated the contributions and power of women. At the Assembly, the women decided to field a candidate for this leadership role and we offered one of the finest and most competent women in the ecumenical movement, Janice Love, to be considered. We were clear that she will not actively seek the post; the lobbying was done behind the scenes but with the full knowledge of the senior staff and leaders. We were broken when they opted to keep a male ecclesiastical head who had already served for two terms (fourteen years) but represented a constituency that needed to be given the position. We were unable to convince the WCC that women can take up this leadership role and make a difference. This was devastating for women at the Assembly—a feeling of despair that things have not changed in the ecumenical movement, despite a Decade; and after over sixty years of women's committed contributions to WCC's history.

Perhaps, there is some truth in the strong words of concern from Janet Crawford, a long-time participant in the work of the WCC both in the Faith and Order Program and in the Women's program.

> Their (women's) presence is scarcely visible in most official records and in histories which have been written so far. There is little, if any, women's tradition within the WCC, no sense of building on foundations which have already been established, little knowledge of the efforts and achievements of women in the past, little memory of women leaders, and yet, as this work documents women have participated in the WCC from the beginning.[3]

In her research, Janet Crawford focuses on the "'restoration of women to ecumenical memory' and to the understanding that the history of the WCC is a history of women and men working together for the unity and renewal of the church and the human community."[4]

THE LETTER FROM THE FESTIVAL TO THE CHURCHES

"From solidarity to accountability" had been the rallying cry of Musimbi Kanyoro when she preached at the opening worship of the Decade Festival. It was this spirit that compelled the group of women with a few men who were in the drafting group at the Festival, to take the decision to draft a letter to the churches gathered in the Assembly.[5] They represented the feeling of despair and restlessness of many women at the end of a Decade, that only sustained action would move the churches to accountability. In view of this, the drafters addressed an open letter to the churches that communicated women's genuine concerns that enough had not been done to improve the role and participation of women. However, to be able to work on a fully agreed text in a gathering of 2000 people in a very short period of time was an unworkable ecumenical proposition. Despite the many rounds of discussion of a text in the plenary of the Festival, the final text which was then presented at the Eighth Assembly of the WCC was not satisfactory to all. There was not enough time to get it right, so the decision was taken to go with the majority opinion and the letter was presented at the Decade celebratory plenary at the Assembly.

After a decade of committed engagement and many attempts at building solidarity among women, a small group of women at the Festival, found in the letter one phrase as being unacceptable—the affirmation of "human sexuality in all its diversity." One young woman went to the extent of deciding to change her own speech at the Decade plenary of the Assembly—she wanted to add a sentence that implied that we as women came out of the Festival more divided than we went in. It took us many hours of dialogue with her. For this I turned to the skillful woman leader and ecumenist, Janice Love for advice and she joined me in entreating the young woman to not say what she was threatening to say to the gathered churches. After the careful way in which the WCC's women's program had made attempts to bridge the gaps and enable Orthodox Christian women to participate fully in the work of the WCC, it was disheartening because her statement would have shattered those fragile dreams. She finally conceded and deleted that sentence from her intervention; though she did say to the plenary that the final text of the letter did not reflect full consensus in all aspects of moral and theological positions, especially concerning reproductive rights.[6] The Policy Reference Committee II of the Assembly remarked,

> In response to the Decade presentation, some assembly voices expressed differing and even conflicting views. Some voices say "not now, not ever" to issues raised with regard to ordination,

133

sexual orientation, reproductive rights and inclusive language. One speaker expressed this with the thought that "sometimes it seems we are on a different apostolic journey."

Other voices cautioned the assembly about the delay in removing obstacles to the full inclusion of women in every aspect of life, both in the church and in society. These voices say it is time to move on from solidarity to accountability. They state that there is no turning back in the journey of faith that has marked the Decade. This is God's time, God's kairos for transformation.[7]

The second reaction that the Festival letter provoked came a few weeks after the Assembly in the form of a letter addressed to the General Secretary of the WCC from women of the Anglican Church in Britain. I refer to this letter in the earlier chapter of this book on ordination of women to priesthood. Their point of contention was this sentence in the Festival letter:

We recognize that there are a number of ethical and theological issues such as ordination of women, abortion, divorce, human sexuality in all its diversity that have implications for participation and are difficult to address in the church community.[8]

Women from churches where ordination of women is a given; or where it is in discussion; or where women's vocation to ordained ministry had been won after a long hard struggle—objected strongly to this sentence even during the discussion on the letter at the Festival. They argued that it is unjust and theologically incorrect to include the question of ordination of women among a list of issues that have "implications for participation and are difficult to address."[9] The pain that came through their words of protest is fresh in my mind. It did give the Women's Program of the WCC the opportunity to encourage the Faith and Order Movement to take this discussion forward.

At the Decade Festival, the wonderful spirit of joy and camaraderie that had filled that gymnasium seemed to dissipate when the focus shifted to the words and formulations of the letter to the Assembly; some sixty women lined up in front of the microphone to propose amendments. The friendships formed and more importantly the common commitments made to challenge the church to stay in solidarity with women; the commitment to fight all forms of injustice—suddenly seemed to take a back seat. The focus of the Festival shifted to the words of a document which unfortunately had little value beyond the Decade Festival. It is printed here and there; it is included in the official report of the Assembly listed among "Additional Documents."[10] In its report, the Policy Reference Committee of the Assembly did ask the members present to share the letter along with other documents of the Decade plenary with member churches. It is a document that women who attended the event would refer to and perhaps even discuss on occasion, but to church leaders, to women in the pew, the letter did not matter—it was a pity that we allowed it to so preoccupy our minds at the Festival.

The drafters of the Festival letter knew that the concerns of many women were not being handled wisely. The lack of time made them take a compromise position. This underlined, once again that trying to draft common and agreed statements in a short space of time and in such a big gathering is not possible, nor is it just or good ecumenical practice. The value of the consensus model of decision making to discuss contentious and sensitive issues also became clear. The consensus model did finally enter the rules of decision making in the WCC.

An aside is necessary here to describe how the consensus model for decision making came on to the procedures of the WCC. Two Orthodox member churches decided to withdraw from the WCC and others were threatening to leave too on the grounds of theological differences. A Special Commission on Orthodox Participation in the WCC was set up in 1988 which "spurred their leaders to express more sharply and persistently their longstanding theological differences with the organization's Protestant majority."[11] Among the issues they highlighted as problematic was the processes of decision making in the WCC's governing bodies. Such voices of protest did come from a few Protestant churches in the Global South too.

After a two-year process, consensus procedures were adopted at the WCC's Central Committee in 2002 to guide its decision making processes. There was a visible increase in the participation of women, youth and others in all discussions since then. This way of deciding allows for minority voices in a debate and voices of dissent to also be recognized and registered. The injustice that prevails in political processes in the world, of the

135

majority or the more powerful and vocal taking control of decision making processes, cannot be replicated in the life of the church community.

Janice Love explains this well:

> Disaffected constituencies commonly call for changes in how organizations make decisions. As a global institution, the formal rules of the WCC seem foreign to many. Formulated when most of its member churches came from Europe and North America and when governing bodies were overwhelmingly male. Some member churches rarely encounter such parliamentary-style politics in their own home settings. Among those that do, many have lamented for years about how such processes force participants into adversarial "yes" and "no" categories when the group often wants to imagine, explore and discuss alternative possibilities. Although many became adept at using the rules, feminists, young people and delegates from Africa, Asia and Latin America have complained, for decades that the WCC rules needed to move away from the model of Western parliaments.[12]

Janice Love does go on to affirm that Western parliamentary democracy had contributed significantly to unblock patterns of domination and authoritarianism and the abuse of power in political processes in society and in the churches too all over the world. However, she was convinced that reform of procedures is of critical importance because the rules of procedure as they existed were cumbersome and unworkable. What she writes is true, especially for an organization as diverse as the WCC, many in committees did not have a clue about the proposition they were voting on. Before they could understand all the nuances of a decision, even on ethical questions, the delegates were called to take a stand, and vote. This left many in the committees floundering. There have been many occasions when young women, or women from the southern hemisphere, would come to me bewildered; or to tell me they voted as their church leaders voted, as they guessed they at least understood what was going on.

There have been voices of dissent to the decisions of the Special Commission on Orthodox Participation in the WCC, the most vocal being Margot Käßmann, who had for over two decades contributed significantly to key decisions affecting the life of women in the WCC, especially in the work on overcoming violence. In a strong article in the *Ecumenical Review* entitled "A Voice of Dissent,"[13] she offers just that. Her main concern was that the report of the Special Commission is "a document of fear that takes great care to establish the boundaries that divide us. It builds fences, rather than tearing them down."[14] Some of her concerns include—the decisions of the Special Commission calling for inter-denominational prayer, rather than ecumenical worship (which in her understanding has been one of the gifts of the WCC to the ecumenical movement). Other concerns include the qualification added to the use of inclusive language, symbols, imagery and rites that they "should cause no offence to any denomination"—these riders she cannot understand as they seem to go against the spirit of the ecumenical movement. She was also concerned with the phrase "a confrontational stance on the question of ordination of women" should not be taken. Do women who are ordained cause offence? she asks. But she also fears that the consensus model of decision making may dull the prophetic edge of the WCC—she sees it as the loss of the power of every individual's right to vote. Her concerns with the changes being ushered in were strong enough for her to resign from the Central Committee of the WCC. Differences of opinion among women have not always been as amicably settled as it was in this case, between Janice Love and Margot Käßmann—there are other examples. As in this case, women in the ecumenical movement ought to support each other, not allow our differences to divide us.

This was a difficult moment for the women in the WCC—women were divided in opinion, and accusations and counter accusations were heaped on each other—but it reflects the challenge we as women have faced but also the hope that we can learn to overcome differences for the up-building of the ecumenical movement. Janice Love and Margot Käßmann had been strong allies and friends in their ecumenical journey and have remained committed to their friendship, though they took differing positions when the consensus model of decision making was approved. Margot Käßmann has stayed solidly committed to the ecumenical movement—her prayer for the WCC is: "May there be courage to confront the powers of violence and injustice. And may it be a platform for Christians to meet and share across the boundaries of culture, nationalism, capitalism and racism that are still so dominant today."[15]

WOMEN'S OPINIONS DO MATTER

Janice Love, in an article that she boldly titles, "From Insults to Inclusion," speaks of ecumenism as a process not a product.

> A practical definition of this sometimes-painful process might be: dialogue despite the offence. Sometimes we may not realize the depth of our differences until we have offended one another, given offences that are perhaps not intended, but which come as a consequence of fully revealing who we are as we seek to embody our faith. . . Yet if those engaged in ecumenical work never experience each other's challenge and, at times, each other's rage, we will never learn to be a part of the same household, in genuine community, delighting and rejoicing in our diversity while healing our divisions.[16]

Belittling of women's experiences and "insulting" their contributions (to use the word Janice Love uses) happens time and again in our churches, and it happens in the ecumenical movement at its highest levels too. Melanie A. May, feminist theologian from the Church of the Brethren in the US records an incident that took place during the Second Assembly of the WCC in Evanston, USA in 1954.[17] Madeline Barot, from France, Executive Secretary of the Commission on the Life and Work of Women was scheduled to report during an evening session that included a packed agenda of reports and other items. Visser't Hooft, the General Secretary, finally announced that Madeleine Barot had proposed that the Assembly "no longer be exposed to the excessive heat of the night." Melanie May writes: 'According to the official report, "the large audience breathed a sigh of gratitude."'[18] Madeleine Barot had in fact conceded to the General Secretary's request for postponement. When she finally addressed the Assembly, Barot declared,

> As long ago as the 1950s, Florence Nightingale said: "I offered the Church my heart, my mind and all my life, but it sent me to do crochet-work in my grandmother's parlor." In many different forms, this is the response which the women of our day still receive in their offers of service in the Church.[19]

Melanie May records: "Barot later commented that this was not an isolated incident. This attitude was often the same: 'Oh, it's only the women. They can wait until after the more interesting and important issues are dealt with.'"[20] Few women have Barot's courage; most would have just remained silent. There are only a few women who will be able to keep speaking when they feel they just must.

Janice Love shares a similar experience that Pauline Webb had when she was Vice Chair of the WCC.

> Near the end of her term, Pauline spoke assertively and passionately in a contentious debate over some controversial issue which was under consideration in a WCC Executive Committee meeting. A male bishop held a very different point of view and was clearly quite disturbed by what Pauline said. He turned to her and declared, "Now, you have really offended me!" Pauline replied with her usual dry wit, "Well, bishop, that's very interesting. You've been offending me for years!"[21]

When I served on the worship committee of the Sixth Assembly of the WCC in Vancouver, 1983, a bishop on the Committee insisted that we could use only the King James's version of the Bible—because using any other "would go against my conscience," he said. I was one of those who had suggested we use a more modern translation of the Bible to ensure that the language is more inclusive and could not but respond to his remark with, "Bishop, I am suggesting this because you know I have a conscience too!"

The challenges we as women face are various and sometimes difficult to bear, as it is women who are so often belittled or ignored. Women who have played leadership roles in the WCC have shared their struggles to be considered as equal partners in a common ministry—transparency is so often missing, and women's leadership is often undermined.

Pauline Webb recalls what Marie Assaad, the first woman Deputy General Secretary in the WCC, who is introduced in the first chapter of this book, shared at a meeting in 1991.

> Feeling literally small of stature in the midst of so many great and powerful men, she said, even the sheer fact of her lack of height and her natural shyness meant that she felt excluded when men either failed to acknowledge her presence or

spoke to her patronizingly, as to a child. Despite her official status in the Council, some church leaders seemed to be unwilling to enter into any serious conversation with her or even hear her when she did venture to make any contribution to a discussion.[22]

Marie Assaad speaks of the lessons she learnt through her experience in the WCC—to allow the Holy Spirit to give women confidence in their God-given gifts; to rely on the support of other women; to check out ideas with other women and find out whether the ideas we bring are as insignificant as some of the men think; and finally, for women to stop being apologetic for not having the same training and experience as men. She is recorded to have said that women fail to realize the strength of what they must give; that they too have wisdom that is deeply theological and deeply significant.[23]

Pauline Webb recognizes that there have been other models of leadership among men in the ecumenical movement, notably M.M. Thomas, from the Mar Thoma Church in India, who demonstrated "how women and men can cooperate with one another in positions of unusual prominence and stress."[24] One of the crucial debates Pauline had to chair was the controversial and unpopular decision for the WCC to fund the then newly formed liberation organization, the African National Congress in South Africa. M.M. Thomas served as Moderator (then called chairman) of the WCC's Central Committee, when Pauline was vice-chairman (as then called). Susannah Herzel describes the relationship of partnership between Pauline Webb and M.M. Thomas.

> Thomas was a chairman who estimated his burden of responsibility with sane soberness, but he did not attempt to protect Pauline from her share of the difficulties. His expectations from women were entirely free from a patronizing attitude. If there was an important or particularly difficult subject for debate on the agenda, he did not suggest that under the circumstances perhaps he should resume the chair. As a result, Pauline chaired some complex and controversial WCC debates.[25]

Despite a few good experiences, such as what Pauline Webb attests to, it has to be acknowledged that it is rare. As we move forward in our search of a roundtable there are many discussions that we have to yet engage in, also with men who will accompany us on this journey. There was the work done from during the Decade of the Churches in Solidarity with Women and in a more intensive way after 2006, of men in solidarity with women and of positive masculinities, under the leadership of Fulata Mbano Moyo—to affirm the contributions of men who were committed to genuinely accompany women and other men in the search for justice for women and a violence free world for the community of women and men.

THE SECULAR WOMEN'S MOVEMENT AND WHAT WE CAN LEARN

The secular feminist movement after the 1970s and 1980s in most parts of the world had begun to speak of a new feminist alternative of solidarity that will transcend the traditional divisions of class, race, gender, sexual identity, or religion that have impacted discussions and movements of women. To this, we could add church traditions when we speak of the ecumenical movement. Women have too often also been co-opted into these divides and therefore have not been able to make an impact on the life-threatening issues that surround us. What is needed is a new political imagination that will inspire us to refuse to be divided. It has to be acknowledged that the WCC's work has not been completely successful in recognizing the diversity of voices (and therefore feminisms) that make the ecumenical movement what it is. We cannot yet claim to be "women in the ecumenical movement." When at a conference of European scholars, a woman from another culture is asked at the end of her speech whether there are any feminists in her church, it underlines that one form of feminism is considered the correct way and anyone who does not fit into that definition is rejected as not being feminist. When a well-qualified woman is denied participation in a process or not considered for a job because it is declared that "for this position we want only the best, we are not looking for gender balance or regional balance"—the assumption is all too clear. Expertise is nestled in some regions and in males—it cannot be found among women; and too often not in women of the Global South. There are differences depending on the regions, church traditions and contexts from which we come, that we ought to recognize, cherish and honor.

141

Earlier in this book, I mentioned that in 1981 at the world conference held in Sheffield on the Community of Women and Men in the Church, there were voices of dissent—differences in the agendas of women in the ecumenical movement were clearly articulated. At Sheffield, the challenge came largely from women from the Global South who were present, who wanted to know how the WCC would support their survival in the context of the increasing stifling of their livelihoods in economies caught in the grip of global capitalism, external debt and unfair trade practices. The delegates from countries in the South made a statement on the floor claiming that their concern was not so much about their participation in the life of the churches—but on their survival in an unequal world. In their statement they said,

> Those of us from the Third World who are here are grateful for the awakening of our awareness to sexism in our own churches. We are here representing two-thirds of the world's women; they are the most exploited people on earth. While we seek to remedy conscious or unconscious sexual discrimination within the fellowship of the church, let us also look for ways to ending the equally sinful exploitation of the powerless by the powerful, whenever that is found . . . . We have been invited here to explore the concept of new community—a new community where there is equality and justice, where there is an equal sharing of resources and responsibilities . . . . We believe that this concept of new community cannot be pursued without including all.[26]

Some at the Sheffield Conference did not want to give the Statement from participants of the Global South any credence, but there was a response from some European women who acknowledged that the Statement made them keenly aware of the differences in women's struggles around the world. They did remind everyone of the existence of pockets of poverty and want in Europe too in the midst of wealth; but also, of the role Europe plays in maintaining some of the injustices in the world. They emphasized the inter-related nature of the struggles of all women and that as the church and women's movements in Europe, their commitment to justice for women is linked with the commitment to change all oppressive structures in Europe and globally. Their statement was also important as they underlined the paramount importance of a commitment to each other as women in the ecumenical movement.[27]

AN AREA OF ENGAGEMENT THAT IS MISSING

An area of work that was missing in the women's program is inter-faith dialogue. Though the WCC has had a consistent commitment to dialogue and cooperation with people of all faiths for many decades—as women in the ecumenical movement, we have not pursued this strongly enough. Today our liberation depends on our solidarity and joint action with women of all faiths, especially women of minority religions in each society. The WCC does work with women of other faiths in some programmatic work, for example, at UN meetings where the WCC's delegation relates with all women in bringing faith perspectives into debates on rights and other international legal issues. But this needs to be taken to a deeper level—we need to take the solidarity among women further.

Diana Eck from Harvard University who was, for many years, Moderator of the WCC's working group on Dialogue acknowledged the marginal presence of women in inter-faith events. She said in one of her reports to the Dialogue Working Group that the WCC "has not done very well in this area of concern."[28] To right this wrong, she along with Wesley Ariarajah, the then Director of the Dialogue program organized an international conference in Toronto, Canada in 1988, bringing together fifty women from eight religious traditions. This had in part been inspired by a paper of Ursula King, titled "Feminism: The Missing Dimension in the Dialogue of Religions" at a conference organized by the Irish School of Ecumenics in 1995. A quote from her paper will suffice to underline what WCC failed to do: "It is evident that apart from a few rare exceptions, feminism remains the missing dimension of dialogue. This could be substantiated by numerous examples, such as the official dialogue activities of the World Council of Churches."[29]

Wesley Ariarajah remarks that her paper "showed how inadequate and tentative even the WCC's efforts have been, and that the whole dialogue enterprise was marked by the absence of women and women's issues."[30] But then, what is of interest to me is his next sentence, "It also meant that the issue of 'dialogue'

143

was absent in much of the radical rethinking going on among women."[31]

He is correct in his critique that the Women's Program did not invest itself in deepening dialogue with women of all faiths—women cannot ignore the importance of this dimension of the community of women in the world today. We should engage with women of other faiths with the awareness of the increasing religious intolerance and growing religious dis-harmony in the day to day life of communities. Women have worked for, in the past and should continue with more commitment than ever before, the bridging of religious divides and the recognition of the urgency for inter-faith cooperation and solidarity (especially with religious minority groups). At the same time, we should engage in inter-faith relations with women from other faiths because regrettably, all our faith traditions have in-built in them justifications for exclusion and have, in one way or the other, been used to legitimize discrimination such as the abhorrent caste system in India, or racism, or cultural superiority and politically and militaristically motivated attitudes of imperialism—and as a corollary, new definitions of "terrorism." There is also the targeted discrimination of women in religious practices, often related to the fear of women's sexuality.

But, at the same time, such a critical dialogical journey will provide us the creative space to discover the liberation potential of all religions and the potential for the ecumenical movement to break us out of exclusive confessional or denominational claims, so we can seek new forms of community, of shared power and of violence-free forms of partnership among women and between women and men.

WOMEN'S THEOLOGICAL AND ECCLESIASTICAL VOICES

We are the church! This was the spirit that I encountered as I traveled all over the world in the context of the Decade. In other words, women are reclaiming their power to engage more fully in the life of the church and to "transform" it. This reformation movement will, in my opinion, be an important chapter in church history. But then, the agenda of women in the ecumenical movement throughout the fifty years of the ecumenical movement was always about the integrity of the church to "be church" in the world. There has always been an attempt to avoid splitting the societal struggles of women, from what could be described as more "churchy" issues. As Janet Crawford reminds us, right from the First Assembly of the WCC in 1948, women had insisted that "the question of women's place in the church was a *theological and ecclesiological issue,* and it had to do with the very nature of the church and their membership in the body of Christ, and that, women's experiences in the churches was not to be ignored."[32]

It would be inaccurate to make a categorical statement that women's theological voices and contributions and new understandings of ecclesiology have been ignored by the WCC (women theologians have been active participants in the theological work of several departments of the WCC, including the Faith and Order Commission). The Ecumenical Institute of the WCC in Bossey, organized a series of significant events during the course of the Decade under the leadership of Ofelia Ortega, Presbyterian from Cuba, who was then working both as a Program Executive in Bossey and with the Ecumenical Theological Education program of the WCC. One of these programs was an international seminar, "Women in Dialogue: Wholeness of Vision towards the 21st Century" organized by the Ecumenical Institute, Bossey in May 1994, with the Women's Programs of the WCC, the World Alliance of Reformed Churches (as the World Communion of Reformed Churches was then called), the Lutheran World Federation and the Conference of European Churches bringing together some fifty women representing all the organizations. There were several powerful and inspiring presentations from various church traditions and the conference concluded with a statement that focused on the hope for a new church. The statement said,

> We have gathered as women to envision a just future in church and society, for women, for men and for children. Much threatens such a future. To create it will be hard work. For the majority of the women on earth, this is first of all the hard work of survival . . .
>
> We are united
> By our solemn rejection of the pervasive growing violence against women in the whole world
> by the hope in the freedom born of faith

in Mary's son, Jesus;
and in our desire for a new, whole community of human
beings,
earth and all creatures within the embrace of God.[33]

However, by and large, as long as the women's program focused attention on what was deemed "societal" issues such as violence against women, the feminization of poverty, or women
under racism, we were even appreciated—but there was resistance when the women designed a proposal to do a study on
"Women's Voices and Visions of the Church" in response to
what women had said through the Decade. There was concern
that our work would interfere with the work of the Faith and
Order Commission. The concern and question posed by Janet
Crawford as to whether there are "two 'ecclesiological streams'
within the ecumenical movement, a 'women's stream' and a
'Faith and Order stream?'" seemed to hold true.[34] Fortunately, the
then General Secretary, Konrad Raiser, encouraged the plan and
a study was set in place and developed and discussed by women
in the regions and concluded in 2006 at the Assembly in Porto
Alegre. There were a series of publications which record discussions in all the regions[35] and among women from Orthodox
churches.[36] A significant issue of the *Ecumenical Review* focusing
on the process was also published.[37] In its short life, this project
did ask pertinent questions and did challenge the churches and
the WCC to respond. These words from Mary Tanner sum up
the central challenge well:

> The churches together . . . have the possibility to call one an-
> other to live more faithfully as communities of women and
> men proclaiming wholeness and holiness. The churches have
> the possibility to call one another to live together in unity as
> a community of women and men—*to be the church* as God in-
> tends us to be.[38]

THE CHALLENGE OF BEING AN ECUMENICAL FEMINIST AND NOT GIVING UP

In this chapter, I have described some of the challenges wom-
en face in surviving in a patriarchal church and ecumenical
movement. Why then do we stay in the church and ecumenical
movement? A feminist friend from the women's movement in
India who has, a long time ago, given up on institutional forms

of religion, very seriously asked me why I stay in the church and ecumenical movement, when I shared with her the frustrations I sometimes feel. Her question often comes to my mind. I am sure such doubts entered the minds of Sarah Chakko, Madeline Barot, Pauline Webb, and the host of our mothers in the ecumenical movement whose steps we follow with humility and gratitude. As we wrestle with ourselves and yet participate in the church and the ecumenical movement, I stop myself to recognize and reaffirm that this is our church—and that we must make a small contribution to the ongoing work of the Holy Spirit reflected in the colorful and dynamic history of women in the ecumenical movement. Marga Buhrig (1915-2002), the great ecumenist and feminist theologian from Switzerland who was long associated with the WCC and was its European President (1983-1991), reminds us of the ambivalence some of us women who stay in the church (or ecumenical movement) feel in this situation. I had discussed this with her when we met at the Vancouver Assembly in 1983. She has written,

> Many have already left their church in disappointment and anger because they saw too little or no possibilities of change in it, or because such beginnings as there were had been destroyed again and again. But others—and the author of these lines is one of them—are too deeply attached to their church, or to the Universal Church of Jesus Christ in which they believe, to be able to separate themselves from it.[39]

But, it is an accepted fact that many women "are no longer content to accept office in an unchanged and patriarchally structured Church."[40] This is a reality that has to be reckoned with, and sometimes, I believe, the church prefers to ignore. Of course, I have argued often that it is not women who leave the church—it is the church that leaves women behind. And, in fact many women in the ecumenical movement do not leave, they stay, says Marga Buhrig, including herself, because they are

> too deeply attached to their church, or to the Universal Church of Jesus Christ in which they believe, to be able to separate themselves from it. Their hope is that something new will arise out of the ambivalent situation in which they live and suffer, a Church of all and for all.[41]

Melanie May who had served on the WCC's Faith and Order Commission, claims the church as "her place."

> I stay, and stay committed to the church, because I believe the troubled and tumultuous conjunction—women and church, feminist and church—is not one of my own making, but one born to me at my baptism. My dedication to justice-making as to doxology, to worship as to public witness, is the heartbeat of the body of Christ into which I was received upon my confession of my sins, my renunciation of Satan, and my profession of faith in Christ Jesus. The church is, in other words, **my place.**[42]

Letty Russell, whose theology has been affectionately described as "a churchly feminist theology of liberation,"[43] and who was active in the WCC in several ways, writes,

> It is impossible for me and many other alienated women and men to walk away from the church, however, for it has been the bearer of the story of Jesus Christ and the good news of God's love. It seems rather that we have to sit back and ask ourselves about what is happening among us when two or three gather together in Christ's name and begin to think through possible ways of being church that affirm the full humanity of *all* women and men.[44]

THE RENEWAL OF THE HUMAN COMMUNITY AND THE TRANSFORMATION OF THE CHURCH

The first chapters of this book drew attention to some of the many programs initiated by the WCC that have impacted the lives of women—these few examples stand testimony to the commitment expressed by the WCC to women; and the human and other resources that have been set aside for this work. In speaking of the "success stories," I also emphasize that the women's program is not the only place where the concerns of women were addressed. In some of the work of the WCC, special focus is given to women and specific programs have been formulated accordingly.

Wesley Ariarajah, the then director of the WCC's program on Inter-Religious Dialogue, for example, affirms this commitment to full and equal participation of women and men in church and society was to be applied to WCC's own structures and programs. But then he honestly confesses,

While the commitment is clear and decisive, its implementation in its programmatic life has, for a variety of reasons, been somewhat uneven. Within the dialogue programs of the WCC too we have had, and still have, some very effective women's participation, but the overall record remains poor. [45]

IDENTITY AND POWER WITHIN THE COMMUNITY OF WOMEN IN THE CHURCH AND ECUMENICAL MOVEMENT

I here turn to some of the discussions in feminist theory to explore a way forward for the renewal of the women's movement in the ecumenical movement to reach that point when all women can speak of feeling a sense of belonging to the community of women and men in the church and in the ecumenical movement; in the fullest and most complete sense. To do this, it will be important to address questions of identity and power within the community of women and between women and men in the ecumenical movement. This conversation I have heard only in the edges of the movement because on the surface, the promotion of the concept of identity appears to promote polarization. On the contrary, I hold that through the self-affirmation of each one's specific identity, the bonds in a community are strengthened rather than leading to fragmentation and instability. Tensions and a sense of exclusion are more likely to occur only when the differences of each identity are ignored and "harmonizing" strategies are forced on to the community. Identity relates to self-image (a woman's mental model of herself), self-esteem, and individuality—an awareness of oneself in a community. There is of course the danger of creating a hierarchy of identities giving some a sense of superiority over others and of sanctioning through anthropological or theological arguments, the superiority of one identity over another. We need to heed the wisdom embedded in the African saying—"I am because you are"—which stresses that our identities are intertwined and that our identity/humanity has meaning only when the other's identity/humanity can also be respected and honored.

Gender has been a powerful and pervasive force in organizing society. Sociologists often use the term to describe social identity, or the collection of group memberships that define the individual. The French philosopher and psychologist, Michel Foucault,[46] is perhaps the best known for having explored many dimensions of how power politics is played out in gender relationships in all our societies. Foucault does not treat "power" in the conventional way, as it concentrates on powerful individuals and repressive institutions, but as power that reaches into the lives of individuals and society influencing attitudes, discourses, knowledge systems and everyday life. Feminist theologians have drawn inspiration from Foucault's interpretations of power.

Denise Ackerman, for instance, writes,

> The asymmetry of power between women and men has informed feminist analyses and conceptions of history, uncovering gender as a powerful and pervasive force in the organizing of society. Feminists seeking to unmask discriminatory and oppressive views and practices with regard to women, use the concept of "patriarchy," understood as the systematic exercise of male power in all spheres of life, to seek the transformation of society from historically entrenched, unequal relations to a redistribution of power.[47]

One has to accept that it is this which is at the heart of the terrible forms of violence women experience in our world today in the context of war and of peace; in society and family; it is at the heart of the feminization of poverty; and it has legitimized many discriminatory practices against women and has ascribed power and privilege to men over women (and of some women over other women), not just in political and economic institutions but even in the church and the ecumenical movement.

It is time women in the ecumenical movement discussed the many dimensions of this reality. We must interrogate the "limited" understanding of how identity and power operates in our churches and ecumenical movement as defined by using the term "gender" as a political construct. In my understanding, it is unproductive to reduce our discourse to the power relations between women and men and would agree with Ackermann that, "A critique of this analysis is that it can lead to a dichotomous view of the individual vis-à-vis society, as of powerful men vis-à-vis powerless women. Women can become an undifferentiated category to whom passivity is imputed."[48]

Sharon D. Welch draws attention to the fact that though Foucault does not refer to women's experiences in most of his writings, he does state that the women's liberation movement is one of the few genuinely transformative forms of political expression.[49] It is this transformative power of the women's movement that we need to address in the ecumenical movement too—and to do it we need to take a self-critical approach—mutual challenge and correction are the key words here.

There is a danger in speaking of all women as one category as we have too often done in the ecumenical movement. Essentialism tends to make some women's historical subordination to men and their sub-ordination to other women, seem like a natural fact rather than as a cultural, religious, economic and political product. In all our societies, churches and even in the ecumenical movement there are divisions based on race/caste, ethnicity and class, and church traditions and histories—ignoring this would not do justice to the contributions the women's movement can make to challenge the complex power dynamics of patriarchal power as it destroys human life in general and more specifically, women's lives—"overemphasis on individualistic female subjectivity may sometimes overshadow other power dynamics."[50]

Ackermann continues, "Analyses of women's experience of power should uncover both women's collusion with the forces that sustain power as domination over them and their domination over others."[51] I have often asked myself why the many forms of "feminisms" that exist in the Global South are not easily recognized as "feminist." Is it because our questions as well as our methodologies for achieving liberation are different, that makes some brands of feminist consciousness un-recognizable in dominant feminist movements? Can we not simply acknowledge the existence of many "feminisms" in our world—all pioneered by women passionately committed to justice and dignity for women? Generalizations only aggravate tensions between women.

Additionally, in the ecumenical movement, when discussing power and identity, we need to watch out for the temptation of creating a hierarchy in suffering—as each community of the excluded claim that their suffering is worse than that of the other—to forge links of solidarity and mutual support is difficult if each of us would claim the major share of the resources and political power. This is important at a time when so many

efforts are made to devalue the struggles for justice and dignity. Women of the Global South for example, have been told
that we are being reductionist and elitist when we speak up for
women. Mercy Oduyoye speaks of how "African men insisted that liberation as applied to the African woman was a foreign importation. Some even called it an imperialist trap that
would do Africa no good."[52] As women of the Global South, we
are told that poverty, national liberation, racism, casteism etc.
must come first and that we betray our traditions and cultures
when we speak of the liberation of women. It is urgent, therefore, for us to hold together all movements and all struggles that
would challenge patriarchy and its deep links with histories of
colonialism, imperialism as well as church histories. It is in our
consciousness about "shared victimization"[53] that real solidarity
among us can be nurtured. Then, sisterhood takes on a deeper
meaning than supporting the "weaker" among us, or to "pre-
tend union"[54] among us. Sisterhood is built on the bulwark of
genuine dialogue and solidarity to develop together strategies
for a better world for all.

A holistic and inclusive image of God and of society challenges us to find those round tables that will provide a word of
hope and of challenge to all women and men in the ecumenical
movement. The task of reinterpreting power relations and of
discovering the potential of a new community of women and
men in Christ requires that we together would challenge the
assumption that any universal constructions can be claimed un-
critically. It is imperative that women and men from all parts of
the globe recognize that it is such claims that have legitimized
the denial of the dignity and the value of diversity. Perhaps what
is the most challenging for all of us is to recognize that none of
us hold the final truth—but it is a common quest that we can
engage in together.

SOLIDARITY AND A NEW COMMUNITY

In recent decades, global solidarity for the rights of women has
been growing in strength. There was a burst of energy when the
one billion rising movement was initiated seven years ago; and
when flash mobs danced on public streets for women's rights
in big cities all over the world. Social media sites have been effectively used to give visibility to these movements and to elicit

global support. Mainstream media has ensured that stories such as the rape of a woman in a street in India, or the abduction of children in Nigeria, or the abuse of a wife by a politician or a famous sportsperson in the US or in South Africa all got public notice and attention.

Embracing differences will challenge simplistic notions of op-pression as common to all women—a notion that is being rap-idly undermined by the realization that diversity is our strength. But then, we see again and again that patriarchy will use any methodology to keep us divided—this weakens us and therefore this we must diligently watch out for. The urgency for encoun-ters and dialogue among women and men to build a spirit of mutual acceptance and respect across patriarchal divides cannot be postponed. Likewise, in the ecumenical context, genuine and respectful dialogue among women of various church families is of critical importance to build a community of women in the ecumenical movement. It is only then, that we can deconstruct some basic oppressive societal, ecclesiological and theological categories that have endowed power and privilege to some and have kept others submerged in silence. There are several imag-es we can evoke for a new paradigm in facing our differences. Elisabetta Donini, a feminist scientist, who teaches physics in the University of Turin, calls for what she terms "pluralist friend-ship" based on a commitment to "a notion of friendship that is not limited to the circle of those we consider like ourselves but is rather nourished by moving in exactly the opposite direction . . . there is no need at all to legitimate the other as "similar to me."[55]

We have Mary Hunt's image of "justice seeking friends" or Letty Russell's image of "the church in the round"—both im-ages rooted in a commitment to work for a new ordering of church and society. I have been particularly drawn by the image of the Circle of Concerned African Women Theologians—an ever-expanding circle of women doing theology for the sake of societal and faith reconstruction.

I believe that women are the hope for the future of the ecu-menical movement and our societies. We have no other choice but to get on with the business of embracing our differences. We cannot divide ourselves and fault each other's positions. After all, we are in the process of developing alternative political, ecclesial and theological paradigms for the strengthening of the ecumenical movement.

We will continue supporting each other in our yearning to be faithful to God's call to serve the churches and the ecumenical movement. We will continue our exploration into what being church means for the world today as we strive for new models of leadership—ready, responsive and courageous; caring, loving and compassionate; inclusive, hospitable and embracing . . . . so that the churches will grow each day in their faithfulness to the triune God in whom we find our unity.

ENDNOTES

[1] Pauline Webb, *She Flies Beyond. Memories and Hopes of Women in the Ecumenical Movement*, RISK Book Series (Geneva: WCC Publications, 1993), xi. To quote Pauline to lead into the last chapter of this book is of special significance to me. She has been an inspiration and has accompanied me in many ways throughout my sojourn with the WCC—through many conversations and personal email exchanges. The hug of congratulations she gave me at the end of the Decade Festival in 1998 has endured with me and kept me going on my ecumenical journey. I am grateful that I could visit her, in her home a few months before she passed away.

[2] See for instance, Natalie Maxson, *Journey for Justice: The Story of Women in the Ecumenical Movement* (Geneva: WCC Publications, 2013).

[3] Janet Crawford, Preface to "Rocking the Boat! Women's Participation in the WCC 1948-1991" (PhD thesis, Victoria University, Wellington, New Zealand 1995).

[4] Janet Crawford, "Rocking the Boat!" 1995.

[5] "From Solidarity to Accountability: A Letter to the 8th Assembly of the World Council of Churches from the women and men of the Decade Festival of the Churches in Solidarity with Women, Harare, Zimbabwe" as reported in *Together on the Way, Official Report of the Eighth Assembly of the World Council of Churches,* ed. Diane Kessler (Geneva: WCC Publications, 1999), 242-243.

[6] "Letter from the Decade Festival," 242-243.

[7] "Voices of the Decade Plenary," as reported in *Together on the Way,* 250.

[8] "Letter from the Decade Festival," *Together on the Way,* 244.

[9] "Letter from the Decade Festival," *Together on the Way,* 244.

[10] "Additional Documents," *Together on the Way, Official Report of the Eighth Assembly of the World Council of Churches,* ed. Diane Kessler (Geneva: WCC Publications, 1999), 242-277.

[11] Janice Love, "Can We All Agree? Governing the WCC by Consensus," *Christian Century* (November 2002), 8.

[12] Janice Love, "Doing Democracy Differently," *The Ecumenical Review* 55, no.1 (January 2003), 73-75.

[13] Margot Käßmann, "A Voice of Dissent: Questioning the Conclusions of the Special Commission on Orthodox Participation in the WCC," *The Ecumenical Review* 55, no. 1 (January 2003), 67-71.

[14] Käßmann, "A Voice of Dissent," 67.

[15] Käßmann, e-mail message to author, September 4, 2009.

[16] Janice Love, "From Insults to Inclusion," *The Ecumenical Review* 50, Issue 3 (July 1998), 375.

[17] Melanie A. May, *Bonds of Unity: Women, Theology and the Worldwide Church,* American Academy of Religion Academy Series, no 65, ed. Susan Thistlethwaite (Atlanta, Georgia: Scholars Press, 1989), 26-27.

[18] *The Evanston Report: The Second Assembly of the World Council of Churches,* 1954, ed. W.A. Visser't Hooft (London: S.C.M. Press, 1955), 2 and 70.

[19] May, *Bonds of Unity,* quoting Madeleine Barot, *Evanston: An Interpretation,* James Hastings Nichols (New York: Harper & Bros., 1955), 27.

[20] May, *Bonds of Unity,* quoting Susannah Herzel, *A Voice for Women: The Women's Department of the World Council of Churches* (Geneva: World Council of Churches, 1981), 27.

[21] Love, "From Insults to Inclusion," 375.

[22] Webb, *She Flies Beyond,* 17.

[23] Webb, *She Flies Beyond,* 18.

[24] Herzel writing about Pauline Webb's experience, *Voice for Women,* 53.

[25] Herzel, *Voice for Women,* 53.

[26] Constance Parvey, ed., "Third World Statement—European Response, *The Community of Women and Men, The Sheffield Report* (Geneva: WCC, 1983), 96.

[27] A European Response, "Third World Statement—European Response," The Sheffield Report, 1983, 99.

[28] Wesley Ariarajah, from the report of Diana Eck to the Dialogue Working Group in Casablanca, Morocco (June 1989), *Not Without My Neighbour: Issues in Interfaith Relations* (Geneva: WCC Publications, 1999), 59.

[29] Ariarajah, quoting from a paper by Ursula King presented at the "Dialogue of Religions," a conference organized by the Irish School of Ecumenics, in Dublin, Ireland in 1995, *Not Without My Neighbour,* 1999, 61.

[30] Ariarajah, *Not Without my Neighbour,* 60.

[31] Ariarajah, *Not Without my Neighbour,* 60.

[32] Crawford, "Women and Ecclesiology: Two Ecumenical Streams?" *The Ecumenical Review* 53, no. 1 (January 2001), 14.

[33] Ofelia Ortega, Aruna Gnanadason, Musimbi Kanyoro, Nyambura Njoroge, Irja Askola, Beate Stierle, "Introduction," *Women's Visions, Theological Reflection, Celebration, Action,* ed. Ofelia Ortega (Geneva: WCC Publications, 1995), x-xi.

[34] Crawford, *The Ecumenical Review* 53, no. 1(January 2001), 22.

[35] Isabel Apawo Phiri and Sarojini Nadar, eds., *On Being Church: African Women's Voices and Visions* (Geneva: World Council of Churches, 2005); Letty M. Russell, J. Shannon Clarkson and Aruna Gnanadason, eds., *Women's Voices and Visions, Reflections from North America* (Geneva: World Council of Churches, 2005); "New Ways of Being Church, Report of the Asian Regional Meeting organized by WCC and CCA," *In God's Image* 23, 1 (January 2001).

[36] Christina Breaban, Sophie Deicha and Eleni Kasselouri-Hatzivassiliadi, eds., *Women's Voices and Visions of the Church: Reflections of Orthodox Women* (Geneva: World Council of Churches, 2006).

[37] *The Ecumenical Review* 53, no. 1 (January 2001).

[38] Mary Tanner, "On Being Church: Some Thoughts Inspired by the Ecumenical Community," *The Ecumenical Review* 53, no. 1 (January 2001), 71.

[39] Marga Buhrig, "The Role of Women in Ecumenical Dialogue," in *Women Invisible in Church and Theology,* eds. Elisabeth Schussler Fiorenza and Mary Collins (Edinburgh, Concilium: Religion in the Eighties, T. & T. Clark, 1985), 97.

[40] Buhrig,"The Role of Women in Ecumenical Dialogue," 97.

[41] Buhrig, "The Role of Women in Ecumenical Dialogue," 97-98.

[42] Melanie May. Unpublished manuscript from the author, of the text of the sermon she preached at the thanksgiving ceremony of farewell to Rev. Jean Audrey Powers on her retirement.

[43] Shawn M. Copeland, "Journeying to the Household of God," *Liberating Eschatology: Essays in Honor of Letty M. Russell,* eds. Farley Margaret A. and Serene Jones (Louisville, Kentucky: Westminster John Knox Press, 1999), 28.

[44] Russell, "Journeying to the Household of God," 253. Emphasis added.

[45] Ariarajah, "Women and Dialogue: Is Dialogue Compromised?" *Not Without My Neighbour: Issues in Interfaith Relations,* Risk Series (Geneva: WCC Publications, 1999), 59.

[46] See Michel Foucault, *Power, Knowledge: Selected Interviews & Other Writings 1972-1977,* ed. Colin Gordon (New York: Pantheon Books 1980).

[47] Denise M. Ackerman, "Power," *Dictionary of Feminist Theologies,* eds. Letty M. Russell and Shannon J. Clarkson (Louisville, Kentucky: Westminster John Knox Press 1996), 220.

[48] Ackerman, "Power," 220.

[49] Sharon D. Welch, *A Feminist Ethic of Risk.* Revised ed. (Minneapolis: Fortress Press, 2000), 146.

[50] Serene Jones, *Feminist Theory and Christian Theology: Cartographies of Grace* (Minneapolis: Fortress Press, 2000), 29.

[51] Ackerman, "Power," 221.

[52] Mercy Amba Oduyoye, *Daughters of Anowa: African Women and Patriarchy* (Maryknoll, New York: Orbis Books, 1995), 3.

[53] Bell Hooks, *Feminist Theory from Margin to Center* (Boston: Southend Press, 1984), 62.

[54] Hooks, *Feminist Theory from Margin to Center*, 63.

[55] Elisabetta Donini, "Women and a Politics of Diversity," *Ecofeminism and Theology*, Yearbook of the European Society of Women in Theological Research, Germany/Netherlands, 2/1994, 65.

SELECT BIBLIOGRAPHY

Ackerman, Denise, Jonathan A. Draper and Emma Mashinini, eds. *Women Hold up Half the Sky: Women in the Church in Southern Africa.* Pietermaritzburg: Cluster Publications, 1991.

Allan, Gail. *Piecing Hope: The Ecumenical Decade of Churches in Solidarity with Women and Justice for Women in Canada.* DTh thesis, Emmanuel College/Victoria University and the University of Toronto. 2004. Unpublished manuscript shared by the writer with the author, June 2013.

Antone, Hope, ed. *New Ways of Being Church, Report of the Asian Regional Meeting organized by WCC and CCA.* In God's Image, Volume 23:1 (January 2001).

Ariarajah, Wesley. *Did I Betray the Gospel? The Letters of Paul and the Place of Women.* Geneva: WCC Publications, 1996.

Ariarajah, Wesley. *Not Without My Neighbour: Issues in Interfaith Relations.* Geneva: WCC Publications, 1999.

Behr-Sigel, Elisabeth and Kallistos Ware. *The Ordination of Women in the Orthodox Church.* Geneva: WCC Publications, 2000.

Behr-Sigel, Elisabeth. *The Ministry of Women in the Church.* California: Oakwood Publications (published first in French in 1987).

Bent, Ans J. Van der. *Vital Ecumenical Concerns, Sixteen Documentary Surveys.* Geneva: WCC Publications, 1986.

Best, Thomas F. and Martin Robra, eds. *Ecclesiology and Ethics: Ecumenical Ethical Engagement, Moral Formation and the Nature of the Church.* Geneva: WCC Publications, 1997.

Crawford, Janet and Michael Kinnamon. *In God's Image: Reflections on Identity, Human Wholeness and the Authority of Scripture.* Geneva: WCC Publication, 1983.

Crawford, Janet. *Rocking the Boat! Women's Participation in the WCC 1948-1991.* PhD thesis, Victoria University, Wellington New Zealand, 1995.

Ecofeminism and Theology. Yearbook of the European Society of Women in Theological Research, Germany/Netherlands, 2/1994.

Eschle, Catherine. *Global Democracy, Social Movements and Feminism.* Colorado, USA and Oxford, UK: Westview Press, 2001.

Farley, Margaret A. and Serene Jones, eds. *Liberating Eschatology: Essays in Honor of Letty M. Russell.* Louisville, Kentucky: Westminster John Knox Press, 1999.

Fitzgerald, Kyriaki Karidoyanes, ed. *Orthodox Women Speak: Discerning the Signs of the Times.* Geneva: WCC Publications; Brookline Mass.: Holy Cross Orthodox Press, 1999.

Fitzgerald, Kyriaki Karidoyanes. *Women Deacons in the Orthodox Church, Called to Holiness and Ministry.* Second Edition. Massachusetts: Holy Cross Orthodox Press, 1999.

Foucault, Michel. *Power, Knowledge: Selected Interviews & Other Writings 1972-1977,* edited by Colin Gordon. New York: Pantheon Books, 1980.

Gnanadason, Aruna. *Listen to the Women! Listen to the Earth!* Geneva: WCC Publications, 2005.

Gnanadason, Aruna. *No Longer a Secret, The Church and Violence Against Women,* Revised Edition. Geneva: RISK Books, World Council of Churches Publication, 1997.

Hammar, Anna Karin. "After Forty Years—Churches in Solidarity with Women?" *The Ecumenical Review* 40, nos. 3–4, 1988.

Herzel, Susannah. *A Voice for Women: The Women's Department of the World Council of Churches.* Geneva: Women in Church and Society, World Council of Churches, 1981.

Hooks, Bell. *Feminist Theory from Margin to Center.* Boston: Southend Press, 1984.

Hunt, Mary. *Fierce Tenderness: A Feminist Theology of Friendship.* New York: Crossroad, 1992.

Isabel Apawo Phiri and Sarojini Nadar, eds. *On Being Church: African Women's Voices and Visions.* Geneva: World Council of Churches, 2005.

Jones, Serene. *Feminist Theory and Christian Theology: Cartographies of Grace.* Minneapolis: Fortress Press, 2000.

Käßmann, Margot. *Overcoming Violence: The Challenge to the Churches in All Places.* Geneva: WCC Publications, 1998.

Käßmann, Margot. "A Voice of Dissent: Questioning the Conclusions of the Special Commission on Orthodox Participation in the WCC," *The Ecumenical Review* 55, no. 1. January 2003.

Kasselouri-Hatzivassiliadi, Eleni, Fulata Mbano Moyo and Aikaterini Pekridou, eds. *Many Women Were Also There—The Participation of Orthodox Women in the Ecumenical Movement.* Geneva: WCC Publications; Volos Greece: Volos Academy for Theological Studies, 2010.

Kessler, Diane, ed. *Together on the Way, Official Report of the Eighth Assembly of the World Council of Churches.* Geneva: WCC Publications, 1999.

King, Ursula, ed. *Feminist Theologies from the Third World: A Reader.* Maryknoll, New York: Orbis Books, 1995.

Konrad, Raiser. "Report of the General Secretary to the VIII Assembly of the WCC, December 1998," *Ecumenical Review, Echoes from the Harare Assembly* 51, no.1, January 1999. Geneva: WCC Publications, 1999.

Kurian, M. *Sarah Chakko: A Voice for Women in the Ecumenical Movement.* Thiruvalla, India: CSS, 1998.

Liveris, Leonie. *Ancient Taboos and Gender Prejudice: Challenges for Orthodox Women and the Church.* Routledge New Critical Thinking in Religion, Theology and Biblical Studies, 2005.

Love, Janice. "Can We All Agree? Governing the WCC by Consensus," *Christian Century.* November 2002.

Love, Janice. "From Insults to Inclusion," *The Ecumenical Review* 50, Issue 3. July 1998.

Love, Janice. "Doing Democracy Differently," *The Ecumenical Review* 55, no.1. January 2003.

Macdonald, Lesley Orr, ed. *In Good Company, Women in the Ministry.* Glasgow: Wild Goose Publications, 1999.

Mahon, Rianne and Fiona Robinson, eds. *Feminist Ethics and Social Policy: Towards a New Global Political Economy of Care.* Vancouver, Canada: UBC Press, 2011.

Maxson, Natalie. *Journey for Justice: The Story of Women in the Ecumenical Movement.* Geneva: WCC Publications, 2013.

May, Melanie A. *Bonds of Unity: Women, Theology and the Worldwide Church.* American Academy of Religion Academy Series, No 65, edited by Susan Thistlethwaite. Atlanta Georgia: Scholars Press, 1989.

Oduyoye, Mercy Amba. "Violence Against Women: Window on Africa," in *Voices from the Third World* (EATWOT), VIII no.1, June 1995.

Oduyoye, Mercy Amba. *Daughters of Anowa: African Women and Patriarchy.* Maryknoll, New York: Orbis Books, 1995.

Oduyoye, Mercy Amba. *Who Will Roll the Stone Away? The Ecumenical Decade of the Churches in Solidarity with Women.* Geneva: WCC Publications, 1990.

Orevillo-Montenegro, Muriel. *The Jesus of Asian Women.* Maryknoll, New York: Orbis Books, 2006.

Ortega, Ofelia, ed. *Women's Visions, Theological Reflection, Celebration, Action.* Geneva: WCC Publications, 1995.

Parvey, Constance F., ed. *Ordination of Women in Ecumenical Perspective,* Postscript, Faith and Order Paper 105. Geneva: World Council of Churches, 1980.

Parvey, Constance F., ed. *The Community of Women and Men, The Sheffield Report.* Geneva: World Council of Churches, 1983.

Paton, David M., ed. *Breaking Barriers, Nairobi 1975: The Official Report of the Fifth Assembly of the World Council of Churches,* Nairobi, November 23–December 10, 1975. London: ISPCK, 1976.

Patterson, Gillian. *Still Flowing: Women, God and Church.* Geneva: WCC Publications, 1999.

Raiser, Elizabeth and Barbara Robra, eds. *With Love and With Passion: Women's Life and Work in the Worldwide Church.* Geneva: WCC Publications, 2001.

Report of a Consultation on *The Ordination of Women: An Ecumenical Problem,* organized by the Department of Faith and Order and the Department on Cooperation of Men and Women. Geneva: World Council of Churches, May 1963.

Report on Sexism in the 1970s: Discrimination Against Women. Geneva: World Council of Churches, 1975.

Reuther, Rosemary Radford. *Introducing Redemption in Christian Feminism,* Introductions to Feminist Theology. Sheffield: Sheffield Academic Press, 1998.

Rose, Mavis. *Freedom from Sanctified Sexism—Women Transforming the Church.* Queensland, Australia: Allira Publications, 1996.

Russell, Letty M., and Shannon J. Clarkson, eds. *Dictionary of Feminist Theologies.* Louisville, Kentucky: Westminster John Knox Press, 1996.

Russell, Letty. *Church in the Round: Feminist Interpretation of the Church.* Louisville, Kentucky: Westminster John Knox Press, 1993.

Russell, Letty. *Household of Freedom, Authority in Feminist Theology.* Louisville, Kentucky: Westminster Press 1987.

Russell, M. Letty, J. Shannon Clarkson and Aruna Gnanadason, eds. *Women's Voices and Visions, Reflections from North America.* Geneva: World Council of Churches, 2005.

Schussler-Fiorenza, Elisabeth and M. Shawn Copeland, eds. *Women Invisible in Church and Theology*. Edinburgh, Concilium 182, Dec. 1/1985. T. & T. Clark, 1985.

Schussler-Fiorenza, Elisabeth and M.Shawn Copeland, eds. *Feminist Theology in Different Contexts*. Concilium 1996/1. Maryknoll, NY: Orbis and London: SCM, 1996.

Schussler-Fiorenza, Elisabeth. *In Memory of Her: A Feminist Theological Reconstruction of Christian Origins*. Reprint, New York: Crossroad, 1983.

The Ecumenical Review 50, nos. 3–4 (July 1988).

The Ecumenical Review 53, no.1 (January 2001).

The Ecumenical Review 54, no.3 (July 2002).

The Ecumenical Review 55, no.1 (January 2003).

The Interim Report of the Study on the Place of Women in the Church. Geneva: World Council of Churches, 1948.

Thrall, M.E. *The Ordination of Women to the Priesthood: A Study of the Biblical Evidence,* Studies in Ministry and Worship. London: SCM Press Ltd. 1958.

Visser't Hooft, Willem A. *The Evanston Report: The Second Assembly of the World Council of Churches, 1954*. London: S.C.M. Press, 1955.

Wartenberg-Potter, Barbel. *We Will Not Hang Our Harps on Willows*: *Global Sisterhood and God's Song*. Translated by Fred Kaan. New York: The Crossroad Publishing Company, 1990.

Webb, Pauline. *She Flies Beyond: Memories and Hopes of Women in the Ecumenical Movement*. RISK Book Series. Geneva: WCC Publications, 1993.

Webb, Pauline. *World Wide Webb: Journeys in Faith and Hope*. London: Canterbury Press Norwich, 2006.

Welch, Sharon D. *A Feminist Ethic of Risk*. Revised Edition. Minneapolis: Fortress Press, 2000.

APPENDIX

INDEX

169